EDUCATION FOR WORLD UNDERSTANDING

by

JAMES L. HENDERSON, M.A., Ph.D.
**Senior Lecturer in History and International Affairs,
Institute of Education, London University**

PERGAMON PRESS
**OXFORD · LONDON · EDINBURGH · NEW YORK
TORONTO · SYDNEY · PARIS · BRAUNSCHWEIG**

PERGAMON PRESS LTD.,
Headington Hill Hall, Oxford
4 & 5 Fitzroy Square, London W.1

PERGAMON PRESS (SCOTLAND) LTD.,
2 & 3 Teviot Place, Edinburgh 1

PERGAMON PRESS INC.,
44–01 21st Street, Long Island City, New York 11101

PERGAMON OF CANADA LTD.,
207 Queen's Quay West, Toronto 1

PERGAMON PRESS (AUST.) PTY. LTD.,
19a Boundary Street, Rushcutters Bay, N.S.W. 2011, Australia

PERGAMON PRESS S.A.R.L.,
24 rue des Écoles, Paris 5e

VIEWEG & SOHN GMBH,
Burgplatz 1, Braunschweig

Copyright © 1968 Pergamon Press Ltd.

First edition 1968

Library of Congress Catalog Card No. 68-8331

Printed in Great Britain by A. Wheaton & Co., Exeter

This book is sold subject to the condition
that it shall not, by way of trade, be lent,
resold, hired out, or otherwise disposed
of without the publisher's consent,
in any form of binding or cover
other than that in which
it is published.

08 013216 2 (flexicover)
08 013217 0 (hard cover)

For my Children

CONTENTS

Acknowledgements		ix
Introduction		1
Chapter 1.	Examples of Collective Action	14
Chapter 2.	Pre-Secondary School Possibilities	28
Chapter 3.	Exercises in Comparative Nationalism	45
Chapter 4.	World Studies	58
	A. At the University	58
	B. Further and Adult Education	69
Chapter 5.	The Terrestrial Teacher	84
Chapter 6.	The Promise of Collective Memories	106
	1. The Refugee Phenomenon	126
	2. The Malaise of Vietnam	139
	3. The Predicament of UNO	144
Appendix	A Pedagogical Exercise in the Presentation of an Historical Conflict Situation	
	St. Thomas More and Thomas Cromwell	149
Suggestions for Further Reading		157
Index		159

ACKNOWLEDGEMENTS

ACKNOWLEDGEMENT is due to the publishers, editors and authors whose material has been reprinted in this volume. The extract from Sir Fred Clarke's *Education and World Order* was published in *International Affairs* vol. 21, by the Royal Institute of International Affairs. Extracts appear from Teilhard de Chardin's *The Future of Man* and *Letters from a Traveller* which were published by Collins. The Observer Foreign News Service first published the articles by John Davy, "Children in Nepal Confound Scientists", and George Black, "Escaping Season Begins in Eastern Europe". An extract appears, reprinted by permission of Coward-McCann, Inc., and Leslie Frewin Ltd., from "The Thought Revolution" by Tung Chi-Ping with Humphrey Evans. Copyright 1966 by Tung Chi-Ping and Humphrey Evans. The extract from Erich Neumann's *The Origins and History of Consciousness* appears by permission of Routledge & Kegan Paul Ltd., and translated by R. F. C. Hull, Bollingen Series XLII, copyright 1954 by Bollingen Foundation, New York. Published for Bollingen Foundation by Princeton University Press. The extract from A. Bozeman's *Politics and Culture in International History* (1960) appears by permission of Princeton University Press. *A Study of War* by Quincy Wright, from which extracts appear, was published by University of Chicago Press, 1964. The extract from Bertrand Russell's *Freedom and Organisation* was published by George Allen & Unwin Ltd. Material from *The Servant of Peace, Dag Hammarskjöld Speeches*, appears by permission of Mr. Bo Hammarskjöld and Mr. Sten Hammarskjöld. The extract from Max Lerner's *America as a Civilisation* appears by permission of Jonathan Cape Ltd., and Simon and Schuster Inc. *The Quality of Education in Developing Countries* by C. E. Beeby was published by Harvard

University Press, 1967. "A Letter by Sir Julian Huxley on Evolution" appeared in *Encounter,* June 1960. The material from Bouquet's *Comparative Religion* was published by Penguin Books Ltd., and from C. Rycroft's *Psycho-analysis Observed* by Constable. *The Times* Leader of 8 April 1967 appears by permission of *The Times.* Richard A. Falk's article "The Revolution in Peace Education" appeared originally in *Saturday Review,* 21 May 1966. Gene Sharp's material appeared in his preface to *The Political Equivalent of War—Civilian Defense,* published by the Carnegie Endowment for International Peace. The talk by Max Kirschner, "Wilful Waste, Woeful Want: India's Agriculture", was printed in the *Listener* of 26 January 1967. The extract from Barton Pike's *Robert Musil: An Introduction to his Work,* © 1961, by Cornell University, is used by permission of Cornell University Press. Material from Thomas Mann's *Dr Faustus,* translated by H. T. Lowe Porter, appears by permission of Martin Secker & Warburg Ltd., and Alfred A. Knopf Inc. Extracts appear from *The Fall* by Albert Camus, copyright © Editions Gallimard (Hamish Hamilton, London, 1957), translated by Stuart Gilbert. Edward Arnold (Publishers) Ltd. gave us permission to reproduce material from E. M. Forster's *A Passage to India.* Extracts from *Between Man and Man* by M. Buber appear by permission of Routledge & Kegan Paul Ltd., and the MacMillan Company.

We thank Methuen & Company Ltd., for permission to reproduce material from Dr. Henderson's book *Since 1945: Aspects of Contemporary History,* and Routledge & Kegan Paul Ltd., and New York: Humanities Press Inc., 1955, for permission to reproduce the extract from *Experiment in Depth* by P. W. Martin. Basil Blackwell hold the copyright of *The Ulysses Theme* by W. B. Stanford, from which an extract appears. The material from "The Allocution" by W. S. Churchill, which prefaced *The Home Letters of T. E. Lawrence and His Brothers,* appears by permission of The Baroness Spencer Churchill of Chartwell. *England Under the Tudors* by A. D. Innes, from which an extract appears, was first published by Methuen & Company Ltd. Odhams Books Ltd. and Harper & Row gave their permission for us to use the extract from Alan Bullock's *Hitler: A Study in Tyranny*. The extract from *Men Against Humanity* by Gabriel Marcel appears by permission of Harvill Press Ltd., and the Henry Regnery Company. We have used material from *Nationalism and Ideology* by Barbara Ward, copyright © 1966, W. W. Norton & Co. Inc. (Hamish Hamilton, London). The extract from *Man in this World* by Hans Zehrer was published by Hodder & Stoughton Ltd. Material from *Vietnam, Lotus in a Sea of Fire* by Thich Nhat Hanh appears by permission of S. C. M. Press Ltd., © 1967, by Hill and Wang Inc., reprinted by permission of Hill and Wang. *The Psychological Problem of Disarmament* by Philip Seed, from which an extract appears, was published by Housman's. Eyre & Spottiswoode (Publishers) Ltd. gave permission for us to reproduce the extract from *Maria Theresa: the Last Conservative* by Constance Lily Morris. Material appears with permission of the United Nations High Commissioner for Refugees. Dr. Zimmer's lecture is reproduced by permission of Mrs. Heinrich Zimmer. Morna Stuart gave us permission to reproduce extracts from her play *Traitor's Gate*. Material from *The Man Without Qualities* by Robert Musil appears by permission of Martin Secker & Warburg Ltd. Every effort has been made to trace and acknowledge ownership of copyright. The publishers will be glad to make suitable arrangements with any copyright holders whom it has not been possible to contact.

INTRODUCTION

BECAUSE the survival of the human species depends on the rapid establishment of some degree of world order, the educational foundations for it must be laid now. What can we teach our children that will help them to master the problems involved in creating that order? The answer, which I propose in this book, is tentative, searching, incomplete, but hopeful; it is meant to strike a sympathetic chord, a "Yes, I see what you mean", in the hearts and minds of parents, students and teachers everywhere on this planet.

Such a blueprint for education for world understanding must be valid in any quarter of the globe, however greatly its realisation in practice may have to vary according to the local exigencies of political, economic and cultural pressures. Its characteristics were well described by Sir Fred Clarke in an article entitled "Education and World Order" (*International Affairs*, Vol. 21, p. 3, July 1941):

> I accept without reserve the two propositions which govern the whole enterprise: (1) That the achievement in a workable form of a system of what is known as World Order has now become for us all a matter of extreme urgency; (2) That education, wisely directed, can and must help towards the creation and the maintenance of such a system.
>
> What I cannot accept is the naive notion that all that is needed is formal agreement upon a paper plan, followed by systematic propaganda in schools, colleges and all places of learning, in support of it. One would have thought that experience with the League of Nations would be sufficient to dispose of that visionary hope. The problem is infinitely more complex than that, involving as it does all sorts of subtle and intricate factors of particular histories, school habits and traditions, and the resulting peculiarities of social psychology. Moreover, it is essential that those who approach the problem should do so with some degree of experience, hardly-won it may be, of how human affairs actually proceed. . . .
>
> Our objective might perhaps be defined in some such terms as these: the progressive creation among the world's peoples of a texture of conventions,

attitudes, understandings and mutual tolerances comparable to those the operation of which ensures order, security, cohesion and peaceful intercourse within a single national community. The key word here is community. Indeed, a thorough exploration of its meaning may yield the master key to our whole problem. For it is the stuff of community in wider communality spread, beyond the limit of national barriers, which will fertilise the soil out of which a moral order will grow. The process must already have advanced some way or we could not now be talking seriously about world order at all. . . . We may say then, that what we are concerned with is a bridge-texture of community woven across from nation to nation in continuity with a texture of the same general kind within each national group.

Because the recommendations for creating such a "bridge-texture" are based on a number of specific assumptions, which should be made clear to the reader at the outset, I shall devote these few introductory pages to a description of them.

The first assumption is about the nature of the present world crisis; the second is about the way in which consciousness develops; the third is about the constants and variables in human behaviour; and the fourth is about the meaning of education. All four of these assumptions are plainly open to modification, but the retention of their basic quality is essential to the general sense of my argument.

I. The Nature of the Present World Crisis

Dag Hammarskjöld in a speech at the University of Chicago Law School in 1960 remarked: "Working at the edge of the development of human society is to work on the brink of the unknown. Much of what is done will one day prove to have been of little avail. That is no excuse for the failure to act in accordance with our basic understanding, in recognition of its limits but with faith in the ultimate results of the creative evolution in which it is our privilege to co-operate."

It is this kind of working at the edge of the development of human society that those men and women are doing, who, whatever their type or belief, have recognised the essentials of the crisis, namely that the choice before the species is survival as a unit or extinction as atomic fragments. Standing on that brink of the unknown it is possible to discern the main features of man's present predicament. Their character has been defined by Pierre Teilhard de Chardin in his *The Future of Man*, p. 66: "The phenomenon of growing consciousness on earth, in short, is directly due to the increasingly advanced organisation of more and more complicated elements, successively created by the working of chemistry and life."

This increasingly advanced organisation of more and more complicated elements can be analysed into three interlocking aspects: political, economic and spiritual. Because, in combination, they provide the key to any understanding of the present world crisis, each requires a brief scrutiny.

Politically the dominant fact of today is that the world is composed of more than a hundred sovereign nation states in varying stages of development but all, old and young alike, requiring a supranational context for the solution of their problems. As yet only the United Nations Organisation exists governmentally to secure that context, and events from Suez to Cuba demonstrated its limitations, while peace-keeping in Cyprus and the Middle East illustrates its achievements and frustrations. As one of its historians remarks: "The UN perfectly embodies in institutional form the tragic paradox of our age; it has become indispensable before it has become effective" (H. G. Nicholas, United Nations, *Encounter*, February 1962). Meanwhile the Great Powers continue to menace themselves and others just because of their unbridled sovereignties. Their fingers hover uncertainly over the buttons of the "deterrent", and their policies are big with the menace of ideological conflict.

Economically the world is confronted by the twin-headed problem of food and population. One-tenth of the earth's inhabitants dispose of 80 per cent of the world's income: in 40 years time their number will exceed 6000 million in some such pattern as is shown by the diagram overleaf, and the gap between "have" and "have not" countries widens instead of closing.

Spiritually human beings are composed, as they always have been, of ego-centred personalities ("me in the middle") and power-

ESTIMATE OF WORLD POPULATION INCREASE BY THE YEAR A.D. 2000

In millions	500	1000	1500
Switzerland–			
France —			
Gt. Britain ———			
Italy ——			
Germany ———			
Japan ————			
U.S.A. ———————————			
U.S.S.R. ————————————			
India ————————————————————			
China ————————————————————————			

Adapted from the front-page cover of the *Darmstädter Blätter*.

driven groups, but a uniquely new factor has now been added: whether by choice or necessity they are all in communication with one another, and this is at a time when traditional religious beliefs concerning the fatherhood of God and the brotherhood of Man are on the wane, when class stereotypes are stronger than ever and racial prejudices more acute.

If the diagnosis just offered is at all on the right lines, then the following admonition of Dean Rusk takes on a fearful urgency: "We must alert our young people that the rest of the world will be in our living rooms for the rest of our lives."

In order to do so we must avail ourselves of all the technological expertise we possess and make the fullest possible use of the most recent understanding we have obtained of the springs of human motivation. This means that we must introduce a firm concept of how consciousness in the individual and the group does in fact originate and grow.

II. The Evolution of Consciousness

The word, consciousness, is the name given to that faculty which enables us to say of ourselves, of our neighbours or our environment: "I know that I know myself, you and it: I know that

I am loving, working, playing, that I am not just performing in a kind of stupor as when consciousness is temporarily eclipsed." It is a faculty, which is liable to expansion, contraction and obliteration: it is informed through four main instruments, which may combine in any number of relationships; they are hand (sensation), heart (emotion), head (reason) and "hunch" (intuition). Moreover, consciousness is involved in an extremely delicate biochemical balance that can be easily upset. It is both an individual and a collective faculty, each interacting with the other. Because their joint expansion from the local, national, regional span to the global one is now becoming imperative, it is wise to reflect on how consciousness originated and how it is evolving. Such reflections need to take into account the development of consciousness in relation to external, environmental factors and also in relation to those internal, physiological and psychological factors which influence every form of development. Originally these two largely overlapped, man was in a state of *participation mystique*—there was no sustained sense of differentiation between outside and inside. As Neumann says in his classic work *The Origins and History of Consciousness* (London, 1954):

> This original phase, when consciousness was a sense organ, is marked by the functions of sensation and intuition, i.e. the perceptive functions which are the first to appear both in the development of primitives and in that of the child.
>
> Thus evolving consciousness is at least as much open to internal as to external stimulus. But it is significant that the registering organ which receives these stimuli from inside and outside feels, and necessarily feels, it is remote from them, different, and as it were, extrinsic. It stands like a registration system half way between the external world and the body as a field of inner excitations. This position of detachment is a primary condition of consciousness. . . . (p. 296.)

How then is such a position of detachment attained? C. G. Jung suggests two ways in which consciousness is born:

> The one is a moment of high emotional tension comparable to that scene in Wagner's Parsifal, when Parsifal in the instant of greatest temptation suddenly realises the meaning of Amfortas' wound. The other is a contemplative condition when representations move like dream images (cf. Koestler: *The Act of Creation*). Suddenly an association between two apparently disconnected and remote representations takes

place, through which a great amount of latent energy may be released. Such a moment is a sort of revolution. In each case it is a concentration of energy, arising from an external or internal stimulus that brings about consciousness. (Jung, *Contributions to Analytical Psychology*, p. 365.)

The wound of Amfortas represents symbolically the wound of consciousness. Once afflicted by it, man, whether individually or collectively, has only two choices: either to die of it or to live off it. However, this can take quite contrasting forms.

Two scientists have recently completed studies in the Himalayan kingdom of Nepal. These studies demonstrate cultural differences which amount, in effect, to a different form of consciousness.

Reporting in the Journal SCIENCE, the two scientists—Dr. Francis Dart of Oregon in America, and Dr. Panna Lal Pradhan of Kathmandu in Nepal, describe how they questioned groups of Nepalese children about certain natural phenomena. They asked, for example, "How do you account for rain? Where does rainwater originate? What do most people in the village think about rain? What makes an earthquake?"

In a second group of questions, they sought from the children answers about cause and effect: "How can rainfall be brought about or prevented? Is it appropriate for men to influence the rain? Is there any protection against lightning and thunder?"

A third group of questions related to sources of knowledge: "How were these things learned? How does one know if they are true? How might new knowledge about such things be obtained?"

The children's replies showed, in an often bizarre way, how school learning can lie on top of a much older inheritance—like a separate piecrust.

One group of children when asked about earthquakes, replied: "The earth is supported by four elephants. When one of them shifts the weight to another shoulder an earthquake results." The same children also said: "There are fire and molten lead inside the earth which try to escape. They may crack or move the rock of the earth, causing an earthquake." All agreed that both statements were true.

Similarly, they agreed that lightning came from "the collision of clouds" and from "the bangles of Indra's dancers"; that rain is caused by water vapour cooling, and by gods breaking "vessels of water in the sky".

The Western educator, rooted in his logical culture, may become frustrated at this ability to accept two apparently contradictory statements. But the contradiction, say Dr. Dart and Dr. Pradhan, "is far more apparent to us" than to the children, "who showed no discomfort over it, a fact which should serve to warn the science educator that all is not as it appears on the surface".

Western thought, they say, is now founded on a particular structure of "either–or" logic, quite foreign in many parts of Asia, where philosophy and literature may make great use of paradox. Curiously, modern subatomic physics also demands an abandonment of simple either-or logic, since the student must learn, for instance, that an electron is both a wave and a particle, a notion which might present no difficulty to Nepalese children but which American students, Dr. Dart says, often find extremely difficult to accept.

Another contrast which the scientists note involves the whole nature of knowledge. In the Western world, knowledge is now taken, as a matter of course, to be the fruit of individual hypothesis, leading to personal investigation, checked (and re-checkable at any time) by experiment. This deeply rooted attitude is not now confined to scientists, but is part of the intellectual framework of the whole Western culture.

But the Nepalese were unanimous in saying that the source of knowledge of nature was "books" and "old people". When asked how these obtained their knowledge, the Nepalese replied "from earlier generations of old people" or "from other books".

Occasionally there were references to legends in which some new knowledge was given to man by gods or goddesses. But in general, the Nepalese children's picture of knowledge was of something complete, inherited from the past, not derived from observation and experiment, and rarely capable of being added to. Even knowledge which is obviously "new", such as that necessary for making the transistor radios now familiar in Nepalese villages, was held to be based on knowledge which had always been known by somebody, or else on a special application of old knowledge. The only exception was a boy who tentatively suggested that new knowledge might sometimes come from dreams.

This concept of knowledge as something inherited from the past—never individual or experimental—has shaped education so that it consists mainly of memorising literature and texts by heart. Not unnaturally, Asian students will frequently apply themselves to Western scientific textbooks in the same fashion, and may not easily comprehend the Western demand for questioning and criticism.

Another problem is that some quite difficult intellectual processes of abstraction which become second nature to the Western child at an early age remain quite foreign to the Nepalese studied by Dr. Dart and Dr. Pradhan. This emerged vividly when a group of Nepalese children, and a group of American children, were asked to draw maps of the way from their houses to school. The American 11-year-olds drew conventional abstract maps, showing the route as it would appear from the air, with school and home represented schematically and all the various turnings and cross-roads indicated.

But 15-year-old Nepalese children were not in the habit of imagining a bird's eye view. They represented their immediate experience: they drew *pictures* of home and school, as they appeared from ground level, and simply joined them by a wavy track. The track, say Dr. Dart and Dr. Pradhan, evidently represents "*the process of* going from one to the other", not their spatial relationships.

As the Nepalese children never experience in their familiar surroundings any risk of losing the way, they see no reason to include crossroads, forks, or other navigational clues. And when Nepalese issue directions to a place, they do not describe left and right turns, but list in sequence the landmarks which will actually be encountered.

Thus the whole process of making intellectual models to represent objects or situations, which is so central to Western scientific thought, is quite foreign to the Nepalese. People in the West have forgotten the long and painful struggle, lasting several centuries, which replaced the medieval relationship with nature (which was much more like that of the Nepalese) with the present scientific one.

The early missionary teachers, say Dr. Dart and Dr. Pradhan, tended to assume that they should replace the "primitive" and "decadent" local tradition with the "better", modern Western one. But to force on the Asian or African a strict either–or way of looking at nature and a direct confrontation between the two traditions, invites conflict both within the student's mind and with his elders.

All too often, the two scientists say, this conflict has alienated students from one world "without really admitting to the other". Education should attempt to allow the two traditions to reach an accommodation gradually (as it did in the West), and to encourage children to use their natural curiosity in making observations rather than to learn by heart various scientific "facts and formulas".

Dr. Dart and Dr. Pradhan are developing a new experimental curriculum along these lines. They hope that this may help to produce a real contact between Western and Asian culture.

But they point out that this would mean a full understanding of the fact that, in discussing nature and natural phenomena, an American and a Nepalese may talk about the same things, but from a quite different feeling of what constitutes "reality" and "knowledge". (John Davy, *Children in Nepal Confound Scientists*, O.F.N.S. No. 23591, 28 February 1967.)

Individually then it is those men and women, who in the course of history have attained to a certain level of heightened consciousness that have lived off that wound—a Shakespeare or a Buddha; collectively it is those societies which have blossomed into civilisation and bequeathed their legacies, which others have lived off. Today, if the species is not to die of the contemporary wounds in its consciousness, it must learn how to live off them—in terms of our initial analysis of world crisis, to solve the political, economic and cultural problems which constitute it. In terms of the evolution of consciousness this means reintegrating by means of a universally valid cultural canon the emergence of the unconscious, which can no longer be contained by any of the traditional canons, and which therefore ravages uncanonised through the concentration camps and battlefields of mankind. However, as Neumann reminds us (*op. cit.*, pp. 393–4):

> The civilisation that is about to be born will be a human civilisation in a far higher sense than any has ever been before, as it will have overcome important social, national and racial limitations. . . . Already at a time when the internecine wars of the old canon are still being waged, we can discern, in single individuals, where the synthetic possibilities of the future lie, and almost how it will look. The turning of the mind from the conscious to the unconscious, the responsible rapprochement of human consciousness with the powers of the collective psyche, that is the task of the future. No outward tinkering with the world and no social amelioration can give the quietus to the daemon, to the gods and devils of the human soul, or prevent them from tearing down again and again what consciousness has built. Unless they are assigned their place in consciousness and culture they will never leave mankind in peace. But the preparation for this rapprochement lies, as always, with the hero—the man, in Jung's words "who is caught by the future".

These reflections on the evolution of individual and collective consciousness should have helped to suggest how it has been through the creative tension between archetype and idea within persons and within society that the span of subjective and objective awareness has been stretched. They may serve as a springboard for our next venture, which must be to assess the roles of the archetypal constants and the conceptual variables in human behaviour.

III. *Constants and Variables*

At all times and in all places, just because of his human as distinct from his animal nature, man has required the satisfaction of certain basic needs, especially during the prolonged period of his infant and adolescent dependence on others: these can be summed up as the need to be fed, clothed, housed, loved, to love, to play and to work. These have been common to the twenty-odd civilisations of history as well as to the numerous more elementary societies. On the other hand the manner in which these needs have been expressed and met are infinitely variable—so variable as at times to be self-contradictory or opposed to one another, one man's meat being indeed another man's poison. Similar variables have tended to attract one another and to repel or attract those of a different kind from themselves: contests between them have been either creative or destructive, but never until the middle of this twentieth century have the world's variables been jostled into such close juxtaposition as to confront them with the dread challenge–discover and practise not only those basic constants which unite you as a species but also attain the sophisticated constants, which the very growth of all your different variables have now made imperative. "Grow up or perish"—"One world or none"—these are the popular slogans which portray our human predicament. Just how many variables can twentieth-century man afford without precipitating himself into catastrophic anarchy or genocide? The answer is "a good many" but by no means all, and certainly not some of the prevailing ones such as a gross disparity of variables in living standards between developed and developing economies. In educational terms this means that the world's children of whatever race or colour or creed or class or sex have got to be brought up with a clear and definite understanding of what is a legitimate and realistic balance between the constants and the variables: this understanding will be an amalgam of right thinking and feeling, directed to the fulfilment of three laws dictated by that analysis of the world crisis we have already made. The first law concerns man's need to evolve political institutions, which will make possible the efficient functioning of a world society that has transcended absolute national sovereignties. This means going beyond ideological conflict to a genuine coexistence of political variables, which again implies acceptance of the notion that in any serious dispute "both sides are partly right and partly wrong, and when the rights and wrongs are properly weighed, a third position emerges more adequate than either" (Sabine, *A History of Political Theory*, p. 133).

The second law is that population growth must be controlled and food production and distribution planned on a global basis with due regard to the priority of this form of expenditure of human effort and wealth over other expenditure such as armaments or space travel, however lawful or commendable the latter may in time become. The third law is that man has to rediscover and live from that third element in all human personality, which is the seat of the species' shared value. Although derived from the physical body and conscious reason, from instinct and from ego, it in fact transcends them and can be described as "the mid-point of the personality" (Jung) or as Lewis Mumford once described it "the Self that we share with our fellows". This third law insists that this factor X is recognised and obeyed as the condition of the implementation of the first and second laws:

> There is only one contact charged with an irresistible, centripetal and unifying force and that is contact of the whole of man with the whole of man. (T. de Chardin, *Letters from a Traveller*, p. 139.)

> "Only when nations were found dead-locked in conflict over the interpretation of a value, or in the pursuit of mutually antagonistic goals was it realised that the subscription to internationally approved objectives and methods of obtaining those objectives had not cancelled long standing local value systems and traditional methods of coping with political disputes. (Adda S. Bozeman, *Politics and Culture in International History*, Princeton, U.S.A., 1960.)

Those "long-standing local value systems" are the variables; the "internationally approved objectives" constitute the constants, recognition of which is now the necessary condition of human survival. Education for world understanding consists in bringing up children with sufficient respect for the necessary constants to make possible the creative but disciplined retention of the variables.

IV. The Meaning of Education

Our political, economic and spiritual analysis of world crisis, our reflections on the evolution of consciousness, our definition of constants and variables and the three-fold legislation which they now oblige must next be related to the data of childhood. These consist of four main factors. First, there are the constants of all infancy, namely that not only do all children require the elementary satisfactions of love and security but, as human beings, they all have an in-built predisposition to react on similar lines and largely unconsciously to internal and external stimuli. Secondly, there are the many variables of physical and psychological type. Thirdly, there is the variable of intelligence from the educationally subnormal to the exceptionally gifted. Fourthly, there is the variable of duration and intensity of schooling: the fact that in half of the so-called under-developed countries only 30 per cent of children between 5 and 14 go to school, that in parts of Asia this sinks to 10 per cent and that, for example, in Africa south of the Sahara and north of South Africa only 6000 out of 160 million receive higher education (see Adam Curle, *Educational Strategy for Developing Societies*, Tavistock Publications, 1963). Linked to this fourth factor is the complex problem of education for the masses and education for the élite (in the sense of the leaders): can it have the same basis while inevitably finishing off with very different apices? As we shall be seeing, the answer cannot be a cut and dried one: the human race requires to possess certain skills, information and attitudes, roughly proportionate to the opportunities of the world crisis but realistically attuned to the actual age and aptitudes of individual human beings: only that can be taught which can be learnt.

In the book which follows I shall sketch "a blueprint for an educational system which would encourage the growth of an integrated personality at war neither with itself nor society" (Sir Julian Huxley, *Fawley Lecture*, 1962). My method will be that of "reviving and reactivating those collective memories of mankind that seem to be the most promising sources of international co-operation today, and by recapturing those moments in recorded time in which men of different continents and cultures succeed in transcending their local environments" (Bozeman, *op. cit.*). I shall in the words of the Newsom Report (*Half Our Future*, p. 164) be concerned with "... a whole programme of work designed to set ordinary minds working on world problems".

"In short", as the Director General of UNESCO remarks in his introduction to *The History of Mankind: Cultural and Scientific Development*: "the subject of this work is the gradual development, in its most expressive manifestations of the consciousness of the universal in man."

The success of education for world understanding depends on whether "the consciousness of the universal in man" can be sufficiently widely and rapidly developed.

CHAPTER 1

EXAMPLES OF COLLECTIVE ACTION

WE SHALL now review "certain moments when men of different continents and cultures succeeded in transcending their local environment" (Bozeman, *op. cit.*). This can lead us to consider how due cognisance of the significance of such moments can be built into a programme of education for world understanding. Our examples are drawn from the spheres of war, trade, politics, art, science, sport and religion. In each case an attempt will be made to indicate first the nature of the substantive material, i.e. what has to be known about the subject by the teacher, and secondly possible pedagogical approaches to it.

War

Although paradoxical it is not accidental that this topic should head our list because the primal motive for achieving collective solidarity on however small a basis was to meet a real or imagined threat to a group's security by defensive or offensive violence. Temporary, shifting alliances of tribes to counter a common danger may be regarded as the crude prototype of those certain moments when local environment was transcended—a transcendence which took place for purposes of the hunt, crime and punishment and, it should be further noted, exemplifying the human characteristic that seems to make it easier to combine originally different groups of men in destructive rather than constructive purposes.

As Quincy Wright remarks in his classic, *A Study of War*:

abridged edition; *An Analysis of the Causes, Nature and Control of War*, University of Chicago Press, 1964: "The human species was probably biologically united in its origin and will probably be socially united before its end . . ." (p. 20).

What concerns us here is the intermediate stage when there have been many examples of men of different kinds succeeding in transcending their local environment for the purpose of waging war, quite the most powerful and important of which has been "the nation in arms", a drawing together within a national framework of previously conflicting interests to fight a common foe. Even before the national stage of socio-political grouping, so Marrett writes (*op. cit.*, p. 41):

> It is a commonplace of anthropology that at a certain stage of evolution —the halfway stage, so to speak, war is a prime, civilising agency; in fact, that, as Bagehot puts it: "Civilisation begins because the beginning of civilisation is a military advantage." The reason is not far to seek. "The compact tribe wins," says Bagehot. Or as Spence more elaborately explains, "From the very beginning, the conquest of one people over another has been, in the main, the conquest of the social man over the anti-social man."
> . . . The paradox set forth in connection with primitive war may be recalled. Moderate war is socialising, whereas too much war and war that is too destructive is dis-integrating. With primitive man war made for stability and gradual progress. With civilised man the threshold was passed. (Quincy Wright, p. 50.)

Even comparatively recent wars in the era of nationalism since the fifteenth century can be seen to have served, albeit often at the cost of appalling suffering, such a socialising process. One example is the way in which the faction ridden France of the sixteenth century—that "notable spectacle of our public death" as Montaigne described it—turned via Louis XIV and Napoleon Bonaparte into the modern, more or less integrated nation state. At an even more recent date sovereign nation states got into the habit of forming alliances for specific purposes, e.g. the Grand Alliance against Louis XIV, the Concert of Europe in the nineteenth century, the Allies versus the Central Powers during the First World War (1914–18) and the Coalition against Germany, Italy and Japan in the Second World War (1939–45).

In these cases certainly we have many instances of "men of different cultures and environments succeeding in transcending their local environments"—black men fighting yellow men for white men, Communist and non-Communist democracies combining against Nazi and Fascist totalitarianism. Yet even as this occurred the very nature of war itself changed so completely in quantity as to become something different in quality, namely genocide. In our own day then the threshold, on one side of which war used to serve a useful socialising purpose, has now been crossed for ever. The League of Nations and the United Nations Organisation are symptoms of man's as yet faltering steps to advance into the edifice of organised world peace. "It seems clear that the effort of states to gain security, each through its own sovereignty, under present conditions of economic interdependence and military technique, endangers the sovereignty of many and is hostile to the security of all" (Quincy Wright, *op. cit.*, p. 202). Nevertheless "There has been progress towards a world leadership through international councils, assemblies and commissions with, however, some periods of recession" (Quincy Wright, *op. cit.*, p. 23).

If then in the contemporary world there is no longer a function for war such as it hitherto possessed, the question arises whether and how it can be superseded by an alternative (see Dunn, *Alternatives to War and Violence*). Because the cohesion of a group is strong in proportion as the distinction between the in-group and the out-group is evident, there is the problem of what to do when no human out-group remains, which is today the case in spite of ideological rivalries, for none of the protagonists dare to wage total war. "The world as a whole cannot create a human out-group. Can it make out-groups of impersonal ideas or conditions such as war, disease, unemployment and poverty? Can the preparation for and conduct of a campaign against such an out-group stimulate the discipline, cohesiveness and enthusiasm which war provided in the past?" (Quincy Wright, *op. cit.*, p. 251.)

We shall take up this theme again towards the end of the book. Meanwhile enough has been said to indicate that the history of war, climaxing in the stultification of genocide, can provide valuable insights into some of those "certain moments when men of different continents and cultures succeed in transcending their local environment".

Pedagogically considered, two positive conclusions emerge. The first is that the correct way to approach education for world understanding is by affirming the past socio-political useful function of war in human evolution, not by condemning it as always morally wrong, and then by going on to demonstrate how in our times this previous function no longer exists. The second is that a place must be found in the school curriculum for a study, however modest and elementary of the aetiology of war. This could take the practical form of the systematic study of certain particular wars, each of them illustrating the successive phases of war as a socialising agency and culminating in the enforced rejection of it by mankind as an instrument of policy. An instance of such treatment follows:

(a) A pre-national cohesive grouping of otherwise opposed interests for a common purpose, e.g. the Viking invasions or the Crusades.
(b) National cohesive groupings of otherwise opposed interests for a common purpose, e.g. the War of the Austrian Succession, the Seven Years War or the Crimean War.
(c) National cohesive groupings of otherwise opposed interests for a common purpose, whose means, however, had almost totally begun to pervert their ends, e.g. World Wars I and II.

Such a scheme of study could occupy as much as a year's work or as little as two or three lessons; it could be handled at the 14–16 age level or at the 18–19 age level; it is well documented, and by taking all or any of the topics suggested above, the teacher can by use of the paradigmatic method, enable his pupils to learn about the role of war in human affairs, as one of the springs of collective action, which has now become obsolete.

Trade

Three topics immediately suggest themselves under this heading for substantive and pedagogical treatment. The first of these is the Armaments industry in which undoubtedly "men of different continents and cultures have succeeded in transcending their local environments". Without necessarily subscribing to the theory that the manufacture and sale of armaments are a certain cause, nevertheless wars could not be fought without them; those who invest money in their production do not do so without hope of substantial profit; the markets in which they sell their goods are known to cut across national and even ideological differences, and the encouragement or prohibition of sale is often one of a government's instruments of foreign policy. For example, it was reported in the autumn of 1966 that France was to supply South Africa with sixteen Super-Frelon helicopters costing £500,000 each. These machines can carry thirty troops apiece, plus equipment for minesweeping, anti-submarine detection, their acquisition undoubtedly strengthening the South African Air Force. Yet France is a Western democracy and South Africa is a racist totalitarianism.

On all these grounds the study of a few case histories could be most revealing of a powerful, negative source of human co-operation, the continued existence of which may appear to be tolerable as a mere symptom of international rivalries or proving in the contemporary context so intolerable as to call for its prohibition.

> When Sir Basil Zaharoff wished to make a fortune out of submarines, he failed, at first, with all the Great Powers. But at last he got his compatriots, the Greeks, to take one; this led to the Turks taking two, another Power three, yet another four, and so on to the loss of the Lusitania—a progression wholly agreeable to ship building from first to last. In such a way the investment of new capital came to be bound up with the diplomatic game, and its profits often depended upon the danger of war. (Bertrand Russell, *Freedom and Organisation*, p. 482.)

The story of Krupps offers excellent material for teaching, although it has, of course, its corresponding equivalents in most of the industrialised countries of the world, a fact which receives startling confirmation in the appointment by a Labour Government in Britain of an official arms salesman! From the setting up of the first steel-works in Essen in 1812 for the war against Napoleon there follows a series of colourful Krupps' phenomena, all or any of which can be taken to illustrate a series of lessons on this theme: 1851, the first gun barrel exhibited at the London Exhibition—unsuccessful competition with the rival Armstrong firm in the 1860's, the manufacture of steel armour plating in the 1890's; August 1914, 82,500 employees and 30 per cent of Krupps' output armaments; post-1918 unsuccessful attempts by victorious Allies to destroy the Ruhr armaments industry, unholy alliance with the Soviet Union to supply it with arms in the 1920's and gradual restoration of Krupps' empire, a $10 million loan from the U.S.A., German rearmament under the Nazis; post-1945, second unsuccessful attempt to destroy Krupps, in spite of the dismantling of the works which continued till 1951 and by 1955 with the regaining of sovereignty by the German Federal Republic the whole process once again set in motion. (See Von Klass, *Krupps: the Story of an Industrial Empire*.)

By studying the history of the Krupps family and the way in which the armaments production part of their firm's activities continued to be promoted often against the declared policies of those conducting them, a striking lesson can be learnt and applied to the contemporary scene, e.g.

1. Name the chief armaments manufacturers in the world today.
2. List their main products.
3. Analyse the markets in which they are sold.
4. Find instances of profitable armaments investments dictated by the nature of national foreign policies.
5. Consider the history and problems of disarmament and their implications for education for world understanding.

A second trade topic, illustrating our theme, would be the Hanseatic League. "In the 13th and 14th centuries the whole southern Baltic area, together with the Atlantic sea, as far as the coast of

Britain, was economically united by the great trading organisation of the Hanseatic League, with its most important centres at Lübeck, Danzig and Cologne. London and King's Lynn were thus linked with Sweden and with the Republic of Novgorod in Northern Russia" (J. F. Horrabin, *Atlas of European History*, p. 129).

What were the unifying forces that brought these merchants of many different nationalities together? A common interest in pursuing trade on profitable terms to all, but this must have been backed also by a confidence in one another culturally and even spiritually; another factor was also the absence at first of any strong counter-pull of national allegiances. The evidence, which the Hanse left behind, is still richly available to us in documents and architecture, so providing splendid opportunities for the enterprising teacher to undertake an interdisciplinary approach to a warm, exciting human subject. History, geography, mathematics, economics, art and architecture—all these would have a contribution to make.

A third trade topic could be either the origin and growth of the European Common Market or the Latin American Free Trade Area: Here the motives and mechanisms of trade, already probed in the pre-nationalist era of the Middle Ages, could be reviewed in a contemporary, near post-nationalist epoch in either of two great continental areas. Pedagogically, of the three topics suggested the first would be most suitable for the 15–16 age group, the second for the 12–14 age group and the third for the 16–18 age group.

Politics

There are a number of useful political examples of "certain moments when men of different continents and cultures succeeded in transcending their local environments". The obvious instance is the making of the American nation, while the Swiss Federation might offer a different, smaller scale model. Arising from the former is the particular problem of Civil Rights as a comment on the difficulties of such transcendence where colour is concerned.

Another instance might be the origin and theory of communism—"workers of the world unite"—which contains the notion that the category of workers contains a mystique powerful enough to overwhelm the nationalist allegiances of workers—a theory which recent history only very marginally supports, though examples of it have occurred. Let us therefore consider what pedagogical use for education for world understanding can be made of the forging of the American nation, the awful claims of racism, and the whole question of workers' solidarity.

A quotation from Max Lerner's *America as a Civilisation* (1957) serves well to provide the basic lesson material for the teacher of our theme: "To the heritage of the Indian and Negro cultural strains, of British institutional life, of the Greco-Roman and Judaio-Christian world, of French Revolution doctrine and artistic life, of German romanticism and the political and religious consciousness of 1848 immigration, there was added the whole Mediterranean world, the Slavic, the Celtic Catholics, the Hispanic-American, the Arab-Moslem, the Oriental" (p. 27).

An educational exercise would consist in the systematic identification of each of these items, the meaning of their origin, and their actual incidence on the American continent, the methods, such as the saluting of the Stars and Stripes, employed by successive U.S. governments to cement these heterogeneous groups of immigrants, and the last, most pressing problem of how to come to terms with the substantial Negro portion of the population. In so far as diverse elements have been transcended and a national unity forged out of them, we may here be demonstrating a possible prototype for global unification. The exercise could culminate in a consideration of the validity or otherwise of Victor Hugo's famous prophecy: "I represent a party which does not yet exist: Civilisation. This party will make the 20th century. There will issue from it, first, the United States of Europe and then the United States of the World."

With regard to race, care must be taken, first, to note the legitimate and illegitimate uses of this term; secondly, to illustrate how much the bond of colour is really a bond of common affliction rather than real identification of racial view—with at least until recently a leit-motif being all the non-Whites against the Whites. It is only too painfully easy to select lesson material from almost any part of the world. Starting in the U.S.A., a comparative study could be made between Dr. Luther King's programme and that of the Black Muslims, i.e. racial equality of Black with White versus Black discrimination against White: then the degree of sympathy, large or small between the Negro of the North American continent and the African Negro. Then again the case of South Africa can be taken as a microcosm of the entire problem— Afrikaans versus English, Afrikaan-English Whites versus Bantu, Coloureds and Asiatics. Another example would be the long story of miscegenation in the South American countries and the forging of a native solidarity in the nineteenth-century wars of liberation. The "All-White" Australian policy in face of the "Yellow Peril"— and many other examples are necessarily to be observed in the context of the world's mounting population problem, and the inevitable, not-far-distant eclipse of white domination. Relentlessly the question will be forced out: how far is colour solidarity a real transcendence of local environments or, alternatively, a positive stumbling-block in the path of human co-operation? Robert Gardiner provides a positive reply in his Reith Lectures (*A World of Peoples*, Longmans, 1966), events in the Congo suggest a negative one.

The theory of workers' solidarity was at source one of intellectual conviction, often exemplified in men and women of fanatical zeal such as Lenin or Rosa Luxembourg. It seems so logical, so sweetly reasonable that those who were the essential means of production should and could control the terms on which production functioned. In fact this has not yet been the case in spite of the Bolshevik Revolution of 1917 for a host of reasons to do with the technical and economic complexities of industrialisation and the psychological confusions and reluctances of many involved in it to understand it and to take responsibility for it. Much of the theoretical transcendence can only be relegated to that pathetic field of fantasy, described by Ernst Toller in his *Letters from*

Prison. "An intellectual tore large holes in his coat and trousers. He called this giving his life proletarian aspects." Yet at root the idea is a noble one, not for ever to be gainsaid, and the first half of the twentieth century provided a dramatic example of how a number of men and women, seized of the truth of an ideological conviction, spilt their blood for it in battle. The Spanish Civil War is an eloquent story by means of which the strengths and weaknesses of a particular kind of political transcendence of local environments can be demonstrated to excellent effect in the classroom.

It is, however, when we come to consider the peace-keeping activities of the United Nations Organisation that we find ourselves exactly in the centre of the contemporary, evolutionary phase of political collective action on a world scale. The very imperfections of attempts to realise this so far are in themselves a spur to further action. Therefore any education for world understanding worthy of that name must take compass and cognisance of what has so far been achieved. As Hammarskjöld pointed out in an address at the Law School of Chicago: "In fact, international constitutional law is still in an embryonic stage; we are still in the transition between institutional systems of international coexistence and constitutional systems of international co-operation. . . . Still the nation remains the highest fully organised form for the life of peoples."

Because of this fact the United Nations Organisation exists in a state of "between" and all its peace-keeping activities have been determined by this fact. Nevertheless, there are hard, indisputable pieces of evidence to show that UNO is not static. The following events, which demonstrate the truth of this contention should be the acquired common knowledge of successful collective action that every citizen in the world should possess.

First there is the story of how in 1950 at the time of the Korean conflict, when it looked as if any UN action was going to be prohibited by the use of the veto in the Security Council the effective device was invented, known as the "Uniting for Peace Resolution". This resolution established procedures by which the General

Assembly could take up within 24 hours a question concerning peace and security, whereas a veto by one of the Security Council Great Powers prevented a decision in the Security Council. These procedures were also in fact more or less effective in the Suez, Hungarian, Lebanese and Congo crises.

Secondly, there was the steadily evolving function of the General Secretary, especially with Hammarskjöld, who rightly interpreted his office as being something more than a mere administrator. For example, in 1955 there was his mission to China that resulted in the release of the imprisoned American airmen; there was his organisation and management of the UN Expeditionary Force in Egypt, the strengthening of the UN Observer group in the Lebanon, the creation in 1959 and 1960 of a "UN Presence" in Laos, and finally and for him fatally the Congo operation.

"Naturally", declared Hammarskjöld, "the operation will continue under the previous decision", at a moment when UN action looked like being deadlocked by Soviet hostility, and he successfully resisted attempts made to subdivide his office into a "Troika" or tripartite arrangement.

Thirdly, there is the stirring evidence of how, often under the most appallingly confused conditions, men of different nationalities were able to combine in supra-national units to form both military and civil units in Africa and the Middle East (see Major-General Carl von Horn, *Soldiering for Peace*).

Finally, speaking in soberly realistic terms at a press conference in 1959 Hammarskjöld remarked: "We need a universal organisation, and for that reason the organisation in which we work has to be universal. In that sense, you may see that it is the one—I would not call it hope—method by which we can approach the world peace problem from this angle. Of course, the one hope is that people will show a solid will to compromise, to find ways out of the problems. The United Nations is only an instrument; it is not the creator of politics."

However, the instrument has been used, and that is evidence which can be made use of in education for world understanding, which consists precisely in the forging of that solid will.

Art, Science and Sport

In spite of the vast variety of the world's aesthetic traditions, it is suspiciously easy to find examples of those times when artists of different continents and cultures succeeded in transcending their local environments. Why suspicious? Because the transcendence seems always to take place at the furthest position removed from the facts, political and economic, of so-called real life. The artist's voice speaks above the melée but is only heard by a few and generally only respected by posterity. Nevertheless, some instances of such artistic transcendence undoubtedly demand a place in our curriculum, for example the Romantic Movement in literature, painting and music, which gathered under its mantle devotees from all over Europe, Britain and the U.S.A. A particularly fascinating and useful illustration of it, together with a glimpse of the interaction between literary fiction and stern socio-economic and political reality can be taken from the impact of Sir Walter Scott's *Waverly Novels* on the American "Deep South" in the nineteenth century: "Scott's brand of romanticism made the Southern planter feel like a chivalrous Lord of the Manor." (See R. G. Osterweis, *Romanticism and Nationalism in the Old South*, Yale University Press, 1949.)

Byron's death at Missolonghi and Rupert Brooke's death 100 years later also in Greek waters can be quoted as further evidence of both the artificial and genuine nature of the romantic Anglo-Greek relationship. In even more general terms the essentially European phenomenon of the Romantic Movement with its preoccupation with nationalism and history could be followed through into the Realist and Surrealist aftermaths with their climax in the twentieth century when modern art, especially in its non-representational form, has become a globally understood channel of communication. Henry Moore, Picasso, Kokoschka, Schoenberg, Pasternak, Senghor, Shostakovitch, Ram Gopal, Saul Bellow and Bergman are the voices of twentieth-century man trying to conduct fellow-men beyond the barrier of conceptual thought.

In the case of science two phenomena seem particularly relevant to our purposes. One is the way in which, since the European Renaissance of the sixteenth century until the end of the nineteenth and in spite of intense political nationalist rivalries, scientists the world over freely exchanged information and swapped ideas about their work—a kind of freemasonry of discovery and invention. It was only in our century that political and ideological claims began to put fetters on scientific freedom, climaxing in the dramatic secret struggle for the mastery of nuclear weapons. However, and this is the second of the phenomena, that contest itself gave rise to a reaction both amongst the scientists themselves and in a popular movement: the former is the series of Pugwash Conferences, the latter the Campaign for Nuclear Disarmament. Although neither of these has so far proved effective, the story of each of them is well worth incorporating in our curriculum as examples of attempts to transcend local ideas and allegiances. Pugwash, named after the place of first meeting in the U.S.A. of scientists from all over the world, has given evidence of the socio-political concern felt by such men and women for the use made of what they discover: the Campaign for Nuclear Disarmament was a symptom of the passionate desire of ordinary men and women to break through the terror of the arms race and the threat of the deterrent.

With regard to sport, the idea of a truce to war for the sake of athletic competition dates from the original Olympic Games many hundreds of years ago. Somehow, in spite of countless setbacks and frequent infringements both of the spirit and the letter of this ideal, the ideal has persisted. Sportsmen of the world unite, you have nothing to lose but your races! Yet in spite of the world-wide interest and excitement aroused by sporting events and possibly their long-term ameliorative influence on human behaviour, it must in all realism be admitted that, contrasted with the earlier instances of transcendence such as in war, trade or politics, the sporting idea is a slender one.

Religion

Finally we come to religion: a man's religious beliefs seem to affect him in two ways. Either they conspire to make him fanatical, intolerant, exclusive, in which case his transcendence is achieved over against any of those who do not share his own beliefs; or they link him in charity by means of a sense of mutual involvement in a commonly experienced sense of God or the Holy with all of his fellow men. The Thirty Years War and the persecution of the Jews are examples of the first, the self-sacrificing work of the Quakers, the doctrine and practices of Ahimsa in Hindu tradition are examples of the second. It is from the essentially religious standpoint that "men of different continents and cultures have succeeded in transcending their local environment", for example, the story of Gladys Aylward and the mandarin for whom she was working, and her superb retort to him when unfairly rebuked: "I came to China not to serve you but Jesus Christ."

There is the witness of conscientious objectors to war on religious grounds and the religious bond which grows between men of different faiths when working in the various resistance movements against totalitarian oppression. Some account needs to be given of the work of such bodies as the World Council of Churches and the World Congress of Faiths. As regards pedagogical approach, these and other examples lend themselves to attractive treatment with children of varied ages, intelligences and tastes. Whether as biographical studies or the tracing of movements, the narrative of religious transcendence makes a strong appeal, for it is a common experience of human beings to feel themselves torn between immediate loyalties and goals and "that which concerns them ultimately". The supreme purpose of education for world understanding is to enable men to identify and reverence that which today concerns them all ultimately as human beings. Because such a discovery begins in the years of early childhood, our next chapter is devoted to an explanation of pre-secondary school possibilities.

CHAPTER 2

PRE-SECONDARY SCHOOL POSSIBILITIES

THERE are a number of reasons why this chapter could fairly be described as the most important one in the book. First, the vast majority of the world's children neither receives nor will in the foreseeable future receive more than a pre-secondary education and that, often, of a quite rudimentary nature. Because of inadequacies of selection and provision this category inevitably contains a small but by no means insignificant proportion of highly intelligent pupils deprived of further schooling and therefore constituting a frustrated and potentially disruptive force in any society. Something can and must be done for them by means of further and adult education at a later stage of their lives—a theme to which we shall return. The second reason is that the quality of pre-secondary education, which must be largely concerned with the implanting of basic attitudes and the imparting of elementary skills, is determined much more by the teacher's own grasp of how human nature does in fact develop and by his own maturity than by his academic expertise in a particular subject. A third reason is that it must be carefully determined how far the curriculum of pre-secondary education can be the same for those children who are finished with school at the age of 14 or 15 and for those who continue with it until 18 or 19. A fourth reason is that care must be taken to discriminate between elementary education as it occurs in the context of so-called developed and developing societies.

As a sobering preliminary to discussing the pre-secondary possibilities of education for world understanding, it is wise to take note of the warning and wisdom conveyed by C. E. Beeby in his book *The Quality of Education in Developing Countries* (Harvard University Press 1967). Here he advances the plausible theory that there are detectable four stages of educational growth through which all societies tend to pass in their process of evolution. There are what he calls (1) Dame School, (2) Formalism, (3) Transition, (4) Meaning: the first two are almost entirely dominated by rote-learning, traces of which remain evident even in the fourth and final stage. Pre-secondary education in all developing countries and some so-called developed countries is still and perhaps necessarily a rote-learning form of education. The reasons for this are twofold, "the low-level of the teacher's own education and training and the kinship of educational function and structure to the 'traditional' society, which is custom-bound, hierarchical, prescriptive and unproductive". (Quoted by Beeby on p. 55 of his book from E. G. Hyem's *On the Theory of Social Change*.) Can "innovational" teaching, especially teaching for world understanding, make progress against this?

In proceeding now to assert that it can and must and to outline suggestions with regard to means, the handicaps referred to above should be kept realistically in mind. The proposals which follow must obviously be capable of modification and adaptation to meet the varying circumstances of history, climate, material and cultural sophistication.

If there is to be the minimum necessary amount of linguistic communication between the diverse populations of the world, all children—except for the educationally sub-normal—require to learn two languages, their own mother-tongue and one other as the lingua franca of this planet, Earth. For global convenience, this second language should be and is fast becoming some kind of basic English. With the aid of language laboratory and judicious pupil–teacher exchange schemes, this aim, if generally accepted by mankind, should be realisable in the not far distant future; coupled with this, there should be the fullest possible exploitation of the audio-visual media of communication—the creation of innumerable dialogues between girls and boys of different countries.

Approaching the actual classroom scene, let us now consider

how children between 6 and 15, whether in Moscow or Pekin, London or Lusaka, can be placed in such learning situations as will enable them to grasp the main shaping forces of our time and so to play their part in controlling them. In effect this means sketching the outlines of a syllabus capable of adaptation to meet the requirements of successive age-levels up to the age of about 16 and of wide differences of intelligence.

It should be an acceptable assumption that, during the first three or four years of school life, those children everywhere, who are capable of mastering the elements of reading, writing and number, should become acquainted with three spheres of knowledge. The first of these is the rich legacy of the world's mythology and folklore, partly because of its superb story-appeal at the level of manifest content and partly because through it children can obtain an early view of the recurrent dilemmas of humanity. Such themes of global validity as the mystery of human origin, the quest of the hero and the menace of his antagonist, the high romance of lovers and the dedication of the saint—these are to be found in every culture-pattern and may fittingly be presented as proceeding from one common storehouse of mankind's experience. By way of practical advice two hints may be dropped: one, the excellence of Guerber's *Book of Myths* as source material; two, the value and enjoyment to be obtained from an annual conference of those teachers from many quarters whose especial concern it is to educate this, the youngest age-group.

Next, it is desirable that every child of whatever class or race or creed should be able to make a sensitive and intelligent response to "My People". By this is meant the notion that every human being needs to possess his own special piece of information about that particular In-group into which he happens to have been born. If he is a Jew, he must recollect Israel, if a Welshman the glory of the valleys, if an Indian or Pakistani the sorrowful beauty of Kashmir, if a Negro the turmoil of Harlem or the open spaces of some developing African land, and so on. If taught with love and understanding this lesson need never be "My People, right or wrong" but "My People as one of the human family". It can take the form

PRE-SECONDARY SYLLABUS OF EDUCATION FOR WORLD UNDERSTANDING

Early childhood
  About 6 to 10 years old

| Mythologies and Folk-lore | "My People" | Man's skills
Farming
Building
Machines
Ships
Airplanes |

Young Adolescence
  11 to 15 (A)

| *Government* | *Science* | *Belief* |
| Examples of Kingship, Dictatorship, Democracy | The Story of Evolution

The Story of Communications

The Story of Scientific and Artistic Experiment | Man's Early Pictures of God

Lives of Saintly Men

Values Shared among all men |

Young Adolescence
  11 to 15 (B)

| *Government* | *Science* | *Belief* |
| Tribalism

Early Sophisticated Societies

Feudalism-Slavery

"My Nation"
Organs of World Co-operation | The Scientific Revolutions of the Sixteenth and Seventeenth Centuries
An introduction to the present state of:
1. The Natural Sciences
2. The Social Sciences | The Masks of God
1. Primitive
2. Historical
3. Contemporary |

of a simple, outline narrative with frequent pauses to follow up in detail, when the class's interest indicates, some particularly arresting figure or tantalising predicament—Josephus and the Massacre of Masada, the deeds of Owen Glendower, the wonders of nature in an Indian setting, the rhythm of Jazz or the impressiveness of Kaunda of Zambia.

The third ingredient of any Junior school curriculum, which can be unreservedly recommended as in keeping with our general principle of education for world understanding, is a series of accounts of the development of the chief human skills in both their utilitarian and aesthetic aspects. Here is a possible list: Farming (arable and stock, subsistence and commercial), Architecture (from wigwam to warehouse, chateau or skyscraper, Wren or Gropius), Machines (steam-engines and nuclear reactors), Ships (from canoes to cunarders), Airplanes (towards the achievement of the *Concorde*).

With this kind of triple foundation it should then be possible to construct a further programme of education for world understanding, lasting until about the age of 15 or 16 and operating at two levels of sophistication: (a) for young adolescents of average or less than average ability, (b) for young adolescents of high intelligence. As we shall see, the themes proposed are broadly similar, but their treatment must vary accordingly. Let us set out the syllabus schematically before discussing its dual aspect.

A. 1. *Government*

The concept of a king is not difficult to convey, especially with the help of pictures, stories and poems. In using them, our pedagogical objective will be to establish the function of kingship in various societies and the different ways in which it has been interpreted—sometimes tyrannically, sometimes benevolently. The elements in this figure of father, law-giver and very representative of God on earth, when it comes to the Divine Right of Kings, will be brought out. The role of king as one kind of leader may be sketched and then examples given of how absolute monarchy tended in many parts of Western civilisation to become constitutional monarchy, how finally kings traditionally play authority roles at succeeding stages of a society's development: they are, as it were, the interim focus of its source of order. In lesson presentation, of course, these ideas will almost entirely remain implicit, their truths to be apprehended by the teacher's skilful deployment of such characters as Louis XIV, Queen Tonga, the two English Queen Elizabeths, Philip II, Haile Selassie and many others.

Government by dictatorship may be taken as government in crisis: selection of material should include specimens from the remote past like Sulla, Frederick Barbarossa, Tamurlane, for contrast with the modern variety of dictators such as Mussolini, Hitler, Kemel Atatürk, Stalin.

Here our pedagogical objective is to demonstrate how dictators are brought to power by the unresolved internal conflicts of a society, how their rule may for a time be necessary and legitimate, how it is always short-lived and how most frequently it leads to excesses.

With regard to democracy, this may be presented as the most delicate and difficult of all forms of government, depending for its success on a high degree of maturity in its ruling class, the easy access to and permeation of that class by those previously outside it, a fair degree of economic and military security, and last but certainly not least a more or less consciously held set of shared values among its citizens. With special reference to contemporary differences of definition of democracies, e.g. the People's Democracy of some Communist states and Representative Democracy of some Western states, care should be taken to identify and recognise as legitimate two contrasting emphases—the democracies of the "I" and the democracies of the "we", those whose chief value is attached to the individual and those whose chief value is attached to the collective. It is not hard to prove that these two are only irreconcilable if it is their perversions that we are discussing, namely the irresponsible, anarchic monad or the "ant-heap": true democracy requires respect for individual and collective claims.

Again these ideas, necessarily abstract when briefly summarised as above, need to be presented in terms of practical examples, those from the pupils' own experienced difficulties and delights in their own self-government, and those from history; for example, classical democracy, English and American and Indian democracies. Particular care must be taken to illustrate and explain the decision-making provisions of a democracy, the roles of the committee, the ballot, the control of executive by legislative and judiciary.

As a result of this study of government in its three forms of monarchy, dictatorship and democracy, even the less academically gifted children should have grasped the facts that any kind of society requires government, and that the more responsibly its citizens behave themselves the less need there is for autocratic rule. In world of today, which requires the healthy functioning of a world society with some of the organs of world government, these organs will either function with the free assent and co-operation of mankind as a whole or they will function dictatorially in response to a crisis-state brought about by the planet Earth's inability to recognise its oneness and hence its slither into genocide.

A. 2. Science

Education for world understanding requires some elementary insight from the majority of the coming generation into three great scientific achievements, each of which may be presented in story form. The first of these is the story of evolution, focusing first on the personality of Charles Darwin and then by example, and diagrams indicating that evolution extends to all aspects of life, i.e. not only physiological and biological, but also psychological. The climax to this part of the course would be reached with the explanation that man has now attained a new and unique level of the evolutionary process when he himself has to shoulder responsibility for the nature of its further unfolding. Here too is a splendid opportunity for pointing out that this has got to be a joint enterprise—the species survives or perishes as one.

The text for those teachers responsible for this particular part of the curriculum could be the following words taken from a letter in *Encounter* (June 1960) by Sir Julian Huxley:

> Some general view of human destiny is surely the indispensable educational basis for an unfragmented culture. Yet this task is now largely relegated to the sidelines, often under the head of religious teaching. It could, however, become the unifying core for our educational theory and practice, because at last the increase of our knowledge is providing such a view, both comprehensive and relevant to the present state of the world. The unifying concept is evolution.

This section, too, would be the place for some basic instruction in the nature of race. The main point to be grasped is that racism is a particular symptom of the general unwillingness of human beings to tolerate differences among themselves—in this case the difference of skin colour and physiognomy. The lesson to be rammed home with plentiful examples from a wide variety of situations is the following: whenever social, economic and political conditions are such as conduce to a lowering of reasonably decent standards of human behaviour, men and women regress to a primitive instinctual level, no matter what their colour, when the only way in which they can deal with their sense of inadequacy, weakness and guilt is by projecting it on to others. The demands of the evolutionary process no longer permit of the use of this mechanism. Examples of racial prejudice as obstacles to world understanding may be taken from Smethwick in Britain, Alabama in the U.S.A. or Sharpeville in South Africa.

The second story under our science heading is almost fool-proof: there is abundant, attractive material to be had to demonstrate the many types of human communication: signs, speech, tracks, rivers, seas, roads, canals, railways, ships, airplanes, radio and television stretching out into and utilising the vastness of space. Here our pedagogical problem is once again selection, and this will depend on aim. It is surely to convey to our pupils that man, being a social, a political animal, has always needed to be in communication with his fellows and is always seeking better methods of communication for whatever purpose—commerce, culture and a sheer feeling of human solidarity. It can be shown how from crude, quite local types of communication—the "Bush" telegraph and the "Runner" there has developed instantaneous communication, which too, it must be pointed out, contains risks as well as rewards. What, for example, is the advantage or disadvantage of the ordinary citizen having communicated to him in his home a contemporary battle-scene? Is the "hot" line between Moscow and Washington a better device for international co-operation than a leisurely written ambassadorial report? In order, here as elsewhere, to give concrete reality to the educational programme, the pupils should be given as much practical experience as possible in the actual mechanics of modern communication, for example how radar really works.

This leads straight on to our third story and suggestion, namely the history of the laboratory and the studio. Why does a chemistry or physics laboratory look much the same whether situated in Lesotho or New South Wales? How far do the chemists and physicists working in it resemble one another? They obviously have a common stock of ideas and perform much the same kind of experiments: do they hold the same kind of values? Special attention could be paid to particular scientific discoveries such as penicillin or D.N.A. Here too is an opportunity for discussing the moral and social obligations of scientists: biographical studies are often useful and enjoyable in this context; for example, Rutherford, Oppenheimer, Nils Bohr, Einstein, Freud.

The story of the studio can start in the Lascaux caves, can call in on Leonardo da Vinci in the fifteenth century in Italy, visit a Paris atélier of the Impressionist period, tour the Museum of Modern Art in New York and traffic with the lives and work of a Picasso, Van Gogh, Salvador Dali or a Court painter of the Mogul dynasty in India. What are these artists up to? Is their work a necessity or a luxury for themselves and for us? Why do some works of art last, while others do not? What is the nature of the creative impulse and can we sense it, however faintly on our own pulses? If art is in fact "Eternity protruding into Time" (Rilke), and if aesthetics is "the science of sensuous knowledge" (Baumgarten), then surely we have here an activity common to and available to the whole human species. The exchange and mutual appreciation of past and present art treasures, and the active fostering of this process by children themselves, could be one of the surest aids in education for world understanding. "Art, being in our present epoch of religious and philosophical diversity and atrophy, the most universal, easily understandable language between men of culture all over the world, and so being practically the substitute religion of to-day, is a great winner of souls." (Hendrick Kraemer, *World Cultures and World Religions*, p. 59, Lutterworth Press, 1958.)

A. 3. Belief

The first lesson we have to convey to our pupils here is that from earliest known times evidence exists to indicate that man the world over believed in some kind of power at work in the universe, to which he was subservient: moreover, as can be demonstrated, this belief contained ingredients common to the whole human species. It is probable, and therefore teachable as such, that primitive man's pictures of this power were animistic and polytheistic and only gradually became focused in a monotheistic view. In his useful book on *Comparative Religion* Bouquet describes this situation: "This is the stage of *animatism*, belief in a vague, potent, terrifying, inscrutable Force, which manifests itself in varying degrees and with unequal potency in all types of phenomena, meteorites, bull-roarers, rocks, trees, waterfalls, wild-beasts, blood, eclipses, old men, women, in certain conditions of the sexual life, epileptics and so on" (pp. 41–2). What splendid teaching material there is here in nearly every item of this short-list!

Next, the pupils can be introduced to the idea of the earliest conception of a deity being probably that of the Great Mother, "as we find it among the Aurignacians of, say, 15000 B.C. and later in an almost identical form among the neolithic and early bronze age Mediterranean peoples of Crete, Malta, etc." (*op. cit.*, p. 42).

Two phenomena in early man's beliefs about God can be usefully discussed; the first is the practice of sacrifice as "adoration, thanksgiving, bargaining, propitiation or peace-offering and expiation or reparation" (*op. cit.*, p. 44). What, the teacher may invite his pupils to consider, do we in our little corner of the world "adore, give thanks to, bargain with, propitiate or make reparation to"? The second phenomenon is the sense of that which should and that which should not be done, usually labelled "taboo". Here a valuable exercise can be carried out in listing the various kinds of taboos practised by human beings in the past and today and in trying to see if and when they had a purpose and if they still have a purpose now.

But it is when we come to food that we can demonstrate most cogently one of the basic shared values of mankind and its intimate connection with human attitudes to deity. Why? Because man, then and now, recognises that there is an uncontrolled Power beyond him which he has to court or obey if he wishes to supply his needs.

For example, "Among the Todas of South India and the Bunyoro of Central Africa the important item is milk, and the function of the priest or priest king is to perform such rites as will secure the supply of milk" (p. 48). Above all, eating was the commonest mode of communication with deity, generally by symbolically eating him. Fascinating lesson material may be selected from accounts of the Peruvian August Festival in which a maize loaf was broken up and eaten and this ceremony compared with similar ceremonies in Lithuania, Atlas and Tartary.

Finally a most telling point can be made when demonstrating how the most primitive and the most modern religious faiths have one thing in common, namely that they dispense with precise images of the divine—yet another illustration of one of the guiding themes of the book. For with religion as with everything else the different races of men share unconsciously in certain constants and are now learning to share them consciously: the whole history of the vast interim period is the story of their myriad variable and often contradictory expressions. That story can be graphically retold at greater or shorter length by means of instances taken from a wide variety of polytheistic beliefs.

Against this colourful background of early man's religious enterprise there can now be deployed a series of biographical studies of saintly men—those who were not "softies" as one tough little boy recently called St. Francis of Assisi, but who each in his or her very different ways bear witness to that reality of human experience, which religious people call holiness and the non-religious may be content to call "wholeness". Here is a suggested list, drawn up by using the criteria of wide differences in creed, span, time and type, so offering opportunity for children of multitudinously different characters to find satisfaction in encountering some of them:

Buddha	St. Francis	Socrates
Jesus	St. Bernard	Tagore
Confucius	St. Teresa	
Mohammed	St. Joan	

In considering the last item in this syllabus, the values shared among all men, great care must be taken to claim neither too much nor too little. Against the obvious fact that every human being requires food and shelter and care for his young must be set the stark facts of the gross disparities in the present production and consumption of world food. This basic value can, however, only be claimed to be truly shared when "one man's hunger is literally admitted to be everyone's hunger" and its challenge met by those with full bellies. Once past this prime value, however, it must be admitted that almost all the other values of body and mind are to some extent shared though in vastly different proportions by different races and classes and creeds; nevertheless they as often clash as harmonise with one another, e.g. ideals of physical beauty or culinary tastes. However, if there is to be any hope of global understanding, a permanently uniting value must be identified and satisfied if it exists. Lewis Mumford believes it does: he calls it "The self that we share with our fellows"—that common substratum of humanity which it is possible to point to and contact if we so choose, and which alone seems capable of over-riding cultural and ideological differences. It has various names: the Godhead immanent, the "midpoint of the Personality", the Jewel in the Lotus, the state of Grace or simply Factor X. Its existence cannot be proved but only witnessed to: poignant instances may here most properly be invoked: The Diary of Anne Frank, Oates' self-sacrifice on Scott's last expedition, the wisdom of a Koan, the illumination of tragic drama or music, "cleansing the emotions by pity and fear"—and much nearer home and directly relevant to most young teenagers—the kind of satisfaction and sacrifice offered and made by any truly intimate contact between oneself and another.

Exposed to some such syllabus of Government, Science and Belief between the ages of 11 and 15, it is hard not to conclude that pupils from whatever quarter of the earth will have commonground on which to step and meet.

B. 1.

When indicating how the more highly intelligent, minority section of a world society should be catered for, it will be unnecessary in some sections of the proposed syllabus to go into much detail.

With regard to government, emphasis will at first be on the anthropological and sociological aspects of man's early political development from tribalism via the ancient form of sophisticated societies (city-states and empires) to feudalism. "My Nation" will be a more complex treatment of "My People", previously studied at pre-secondary stage. It should be set firmly in the context of a study of "Comparative Nationalism" (see Chapter 4) and, while given the weight due to its influential rôle in recent and contemporary history, nevertheless be presented as an interim stage in man's socio-political development, now giving way to various forms of world co-operation as stepping-stones to some form eventually of world government.

It is with this point that schools throughout the world have a positively categorical imperative laid on themselves, namely to ensure so far as is humanly possible that their pupils emerge with an excited awareness that they are involved in the actual growth of the organs of world co-operation and especially the United Nations Organisation.

For both the governmental and non-governmental agencies more and more recruits will be required, so that in addition to a general knowledge kind of approach to pupils, there can also be a vocational one—the prospect of some of them making their life careers by working for such bodies. Incidentally it should be noted that it is just as important to know something of the religious, artistic and recreational aspects of their activities as well as of their political and economic ones. A few suggestions for subject matter may be helpful: (1) biographical studies of Trygve Lie, Hammarskjöld and U Thant; (2) studies of one or more of the Peace-keeping activities of UNO, e.g. in Kashmir, Cyprus or the Middle East; (3) a critical appraisal of the Universal Declaration of Human Rights; (4) an evaluation of the work of one of the UN specialised agencies, UNICEF or UNESCO; (5) an estimate of the various politico-economic regional groupings of nations, e.g. GATT, NATO, the Commonwealth, the Common Market. More than a casual glance should be given to and, whenever possible, active participation encouraged in some of the voluntary organisations' activities as themselves contributing to the shaping of a global conscience: the Society of Friends, Christian Aid, I.V.S. are just instances.

B. 2.

Here is the place for a stirring account, truly world-wide though European in origin, of the single greatest shaping force of our times—Science. Beginning with a scrutiny of its origins in Christianity, pupils will then be introduced to the scientific revolutions of the sixteenth and seventeenth centuries—not as a kind of potted, dry-as-dust history of science but as the story of high adventure and daring inside and outside the laboratory: first-hand acquaintance with Newton's *Principia* and Brecht's *Galileo* as well as the careful perusal of Butterfield's great work on *Scientific Revolutions in the 17th Century*. Next, care must be taken to get the nineteenth-century achievements of science in their true perspective as great triumphs based on "materialist" assumptions, followed in the twentieth century by the completely new task given to it in the atomic and post atomic age. For both the Pure and Applied aspects of the subject, valuable aid can be obtained from *Science in its Context*, edited by Brierley (Heinemann) and more obliquely but significantly from Erich Heller's *The Artist's Journey to the Interior*. Again care must be taken to strike a proper balance between the Natural and Social Sciences; for instance, in the case of the latter, the problems and possibilities of automation, computers, controlled genetics and para-pyschology. After their study of this part of the curriculum intelligent 14- and 16-year-olds should have come to accept both the magnitude and limits of what in the following passage is referred to as "the hard, sober, intellectual strength of science": "The truth is that science has developed a conception of hard, sober, intellectual strength that makes mankind's old metaphysical views and moral notions simply unendurable, although all it can put in their place is the hope that a day, still distant, will come when a race of intellectual conquerors will descend into the valleys of spiritual fruitfulness." (Robert Musil, *The Man Without Qualities*, Vol. 1, p. 48.)

B. 3.

The last portion of this course should deal with man's beliefs about first and last things, why he was born and why he must die—"that which concerns him ultimately", to use Tillich's definition of religion. It is around some kind of common belief concerning these matters that the problem of mobilising a new sense of human solidarity becomes manageable.

Joseph Campbell's volumes on *The Masks of God* are an invaluable source for the teacher here. With their help and by reference to selections from the sacred tenets of the great religions and the actual use by the pupils themselves of a book like Bolam and Henderson's *Art and Belief*, it should be possible for boys and girls working at this age and intelligence level to achieve three things:

(1) A sympathetic understanding of what has been called a sense of the "numinous"—the idea of the Holy as first expressed in primitive times and running constantly true to the same patterns in all quarters of the earth—man's trafficking with that which he experiences as "other" to himself and his fellow human beings and yet, paradoxically, most frequently encountered by means of them.

(2) A working knowledge of what the great religions of the world have taught and teach about God and the nature of reality. Here much can be made of the constancy of the Golden Rule as something common to nearly all, although what must also become apparent is the long, sad story of religious intolerance and persecution.

(3) An open-minded attitude of enquiry concerning recent discoveries and revelations in the fields of psychology, physics, chemistry, biology and art, which are beginning to suggest that some modern men at least are beginning to descend by devious routes "into the valleys of spiritual fruitfulness". The kind of things in mind here are the work of C. G. Jung's *Modern Man in Search of a Soul*, Sir Alistair Hardy's *Gifford Lectures* 1965–6 and Sir Herbert Read's *Icon and Idea*. For, as Charles Rycroft observes in *Psycho-analysis Observed* (p. 22),

> ... there would seem to be no necessary incompatibility between psychoanalysis and those religious formulas which locate God within the self. One could indeed argue that Freud's Id (and even Groddeck's It), the impersonal from within which is found the core of oneself and yet not oneself, and from which in illness one becomes alienated, is a secular

formulation of the insight which makes religious people believe in an immanent God: if this was so, psycho-analysis could be regarded as a semantic bridge between science and biology on the one hand and religion and the humanities on the other.

It is our contention that the kind of education for world understanding, sketched in this chapter, could enable teenagers throughout the world to stand and meet on some such bridge.

CHAPTER 3

EXERCISES IN COMPARATIVE NATIONALISM

THE existence of some 150 nation states in the modern world is an obviously relevant fact, which must be taken into account in education for world understanding. In this chapter it will be maintained that a definition of nationalism and an understanding of its dynamics by means of a comparison between different kinds of nations are an essential condition for the modification of their sovereign claims, which if left unmodified present an insurmountable obstacle to the achievement of world order. By a nation-state is understood that form of socio-political organisation, which began to appear in Europe during the fifteenth century, manifested itself in other parts of the world in varying kinds of imperialism, and which has in the twentieth century proliferated everywhere at the very moment when, at any rate in its original structure and intention, it has become an anachronism.

A *Times* Leader of 8 April 1967, gives an admirable description of the depth dimension of nations:

> One of Jung's patients, early in this century, was an American businessman who from early life had entertained the ambition to make a fortune and retire. By the time he was forty he had succeeded; his fortune amounted to several hundred thousand or perhaps a million dollars; he retired to the life of recreation, including fishing and out of doors pursuits, which his heart was set on. Within a few months he suffered a complete mental breakdown, and by the time he reached Jung's consulting room no cure by means then known was possible.
> Jung's diagnosis was that the psychic energy which had been put into the business career had lacked an external outlet in retirement; the result was, as it were, that the energy was transferred inwards and destroyed the man himself. This diagnosis may now seem to be no more than common

sense; we all know the danger that springs from thwarted energy, in ourselves or in other people. In another place Jung comments on the normal consequences: "what we call the 'blocking of libido' is for the primitive, a hard and concrete fact: his life ceases to flow, things lose their glamour, plants, animals, and men no longer prosper. ... Modern man, in the same situation, experiences a standstill (' I am stuck'), a loss of energy and enjoyment ('the zest—libido—have gone out of life') or a depression." He also observes that a blocking of libido leads to "aberrations of all kinds".

One does not need to overestimate the therapeutic efficiency of psychoanalytical theory to recognize that this is a highly interesting comment on the psychological lives of nations. Great nations, that is those with a long history and a strong sense of national identity, need to operate at full stretch, just as able men or fast horses need to do. When they are not working at full stretch, when their energy is diverted from external objects, then they suffer from all sorts of depressions, delusions, and social difficulties. Obvious examples occur in the history of many nations: in British history the most striking instance is the way in which the energies which were used externally in the Hundred Years War turned in upon themselves to produce the national breakdown of the Wars of the Roses.

Equally clearly this problem can now be seen as afflicting each of the major powers of the old Europe, Britain, Germany, and France. These have all three been very great powers; from the mid-seventeenth to the early nineteenth century France dominated Europe, as did Germany from the 1860's to the early 1940's. From the mid-eighteenth to the mid-twentieth century, from Chatham to Churchill, Britain played always a leading and often a dominant role in the rest of the world. Now all three nations are like the retired American businessman; energies which were sufficient to dominate a world are now concentrated on what seems little more than the village green and the parish pump.

Each power has reacted in a different way. France may seem to have escaped, and certainly President de Gaulle has provided an outlet for national pride and for the psychic energy of his country. It is a very great achievement and a real source of his power. Yet the escape is not real, but a fantasy. France, whether seen from Moscow or Washington or London, is not a great power; she is a second class power with pretensions above her real strength. President de Gaulle is not Louis XIV; he is Louis XIV from *son et lumiere*; he is not an expression of the greatness of France, but of the greatness he would like France to have. Like all fantasies this gathers energy to itself, but results in practical decisions being taken which are based on fantasy and not on truth. The French posture in Europe, the French nuclear submarine, are, viewed historically, symbols of detachment from reality.

Germany has followed a different course. The Nazi period, in which at one time German troops had conquered Europe from the Black Sea to the Atlantic, represented a great explosion of psychic energy, but it was a black explosion, in a black cause. The result is that Germany not only suffers from a repression of energy, but from a fear of energy and strong association between national energy and national guilt. Here too there are stirrings of fantasy, and the inevitable stirrings of a desire to find an outward object for national energy, but these stirrings are still for the present largely suppressed.

In Britain, too, one can trace some persistent elements of fantasy, of the belief that past honours can be brought back not through the present but by turning away from the present. A succession of events, of which the Suez crisis was incomparably the most important, has however largely destroyed this fantasy, and British politicians have not, since Sir Winston Churchill, successfully impressed themselves on the public imaginations; we have, for better and for worse, been without great men in the sense that Churchill and de Gaulle have been great men.

The result has been that the three nations have taken three different courses: in France fantasy, in Germany withdrawal and in Britain depression are the most marked symptoms. In France and Germany economic conditions have been very favourable; even in Britain they have been comfortable. It seems clear, however, that affluence, even where it is achieved, does not provide the outlet for energy that is needed.

If there is no external outlet for this energy then deterioration, and possibly dangerous deterioration, seems likely in the morale of all these countries. In France President de Gaulle is not immortal; in Germany there could be a revival of the dark forces; in Britain a continued depression of spirit could lead to social deterioration. What is needed in all these countries is new work to be done. In political terms the work which is open to all three is the remaking of the European community of nations. This is a task which would permit the energies of all the European nations to be used. Because it is an international as well as national task it could be expected to bring out the light rather than the dark side of national energies. And if Europe can be remade, then Europe herself can carry out her own work in helping the rest of the world.

Comparative Nationalism as a subject for study in the higher forms of secondary schools should abide by the following criteria of selection: (1) "My Nation" as the starting-point wherever it happens to be. (2) At least four other nations chosen from contrasting quarters of the earth and, if possible, illustrating "old" and "young" nation states. The following constants of comparison should be applied in each case study: Mode of Origin, Main Features of Development, Present Prospects. Furthermore, under each of these last three headings, approximately constant questions should be asked about the politics, economics and cultures of each particular nation. Through this way of studying recent history, pupils may at least learn sufficient prudence, if without explicit pronouncements of principle, to appreciate the overriding need for supranational contexts for the solution of national problems.

A first study in comparative nationalism might consist in taking the three earliest great nations of Europe—England, France and Spain—and watching their development as imperialist powers with special reference finally to the national liberation of three portions of their former empires, Malawi, Algeria and Mexico.

With regard to England and then Great Britain the salient points to be noted for comparative purposes would be the emergence of Tudor political order after the baronial anarchy of the fifteenth century, the establishment of a prosperous merchant class and the emergence of a national self-consciousness as expressed for example in Shakespeare's lines:

> This happy breed of men, this little world,
> This precious stone set in a silver sea,
> Which serves it in the office of a wall,
> Or as a moat defensive to a house,
> Against the envy of less happier lands;
> This blessed plot, this earth, this realm, this England.
> *(King Richard II*, Act II, Sc. I.)

These are the springs of British nationalism: the dominant features of its development are the political revolution of the seventeenth century, the Industrial Revolution of the late eighteenth and nineteenth centuries and the final phase of conscious imperialism with all that this implies culturally as well as sociopolitically. As to her present prospects as a nation these must be assessed against the background of her altogether changed position in the world since 1945 with loss of Great Power status and the retreat from Empire, part voluntary and part reluctant. In the latter connection will come the study of the national liberation of Nyasaland into Dr. Banda's Malawi. Here again a look must be taken at the origins of this movement from the time of its appearance as a British Protectorate in 1871, its development under the leadership of Dr. Banda up to the acknowledgement of its secession from the Central African Federation in 1962 to its achievement of sovereign nationalism as Malawi in 1964. In this connection it is important to make as scrupulous an assessment as possible of the British imperialist legacy, the degree of economic exploitation and present viability of the country and the nature of the cultural complex, tribal, linguistic, artistic, religious, necessary to its future. Above all the question most burningly alive is whether nationalism as applied to Malawi and nationalism as applied to Great Britain, one the child of the last half-century, the other the child of 400 years, can meaningfully be equated. Are they the same kind of politico-economic-cultural animal? Have they at least in common the fact that in the second half of the twentieth century their viability depends on the degree and manner in which they are integrated into a unit of larger politico-economic design—Pan-Africa, the European Community or even some kind of world federation of states? What is there in common between this first instance of European expansive nationalism and the next?

For the origins of Spanish nationalism we go back to the union of Aragon and Castile and the emergence of Spain as the political premier power of the world in the sixteenth century. Economically the monopoly advantage, though eventually the economic paralysis of the Seville Gold trade, is a key matter together of course with the phase of overseas colonialism in the New World. What finer teaching material could be asked for than the picture of the ageing Philip II in the Escurial and the "Lords of New Spain" carving out principalities and dominions in South America! Then comes the story of the slow decay and petrification of Spain as a European power, compensated for by her achievements in the arts, especially the contribution to world mythology in the figure of Don Quixote of the archetypal anti-hero. The agonising climax of the Spanish study in spent nationalism comes in the twentieth century with the Spanish Civil War, the defeat of the Social Democrats and the dictatorship of Franco for over thirty years—this to be studied in its own right and also as the miniature dress-rehearsal for the clash of the Great Powers in the Second World War.

Then there may be linked to this strikingly clear picture of the rise, fall and renovation in modern form of Spanish nationalism, the story of Mexico—her single greatest overseas enterprise. After a short prologue in brilliant colours of the Aztecs, Mayas and Toltecs lessons can follow on the arrival of the first Spanish ships, the encounter between Montezuma and Cortes and the strange clash religiously between Roman Catholicism and the ancient beliefs of the natives, militarily between modern and outdated weapons of war, administratively between the organisational drive of the European and the loose and shifting structures of the Mexicans themselves, economically the gross exploitation by the Spaniard of his colonies, but also the interpenetration of the two through language and marriage. Next comes the phase of the gradual awakening of the counter-thrust of Mexican nationalism itself with perhaps brief character sketches of Father Hidalyo, Augustin Iturbe, Santa Anna, Benito Juarez, the gorgeous pathetic figures of the Emperor Maximilian and his wife Carlotta. At this point it can be shown how by 1910, ninety years after the overthrow of Spanish rule and thirty years after the rule of their own President Diaz, the Mexican people still lacked any real social amelioration of their lot. In contemplating the challengers to this state of affairs, Francesco Madero and Zapapa and Carranza and Cardinal Aleman, the issue can be finely debated as to the relationship between the forces of national liberation and social reform; are the two necessary concomitants? Do they always mix in the same proportions? What light is thrown on this question from other parts of the world? (See Henderson and Caldwell, *The Chainless Mind*) Culturally, there is the opportunity for exciting media of instruction in the art of mural painting of Diego Rivera and the music of Villa-Lobos. At the end of this second study in European expansive nationalism the question can be naturally posed: Is it possible to strike any kind of debit and credit balance between the colonialists and the people they colonised? If and when contact between previously unconnected portions of the human species came about, was any more just, less wasteful method conceivable? Here, as in the case of Britain and Malawi and, as we shall be seeing, in the case of France and Algeria, one potent and unique factor was at work and probably decisive for the forms which those encounters took, namely the scientific and technical superiority of Europe.

For the origins of French nationalism we go back to the end of the sixteenth century—to the French religious wars. Henry of Navarre's "Paris is worth a mass" was the operative incantation for Louis XIV's "L'État c'est Moi". Politically in the expansion of her frontiers, economically through the achievement of Colbert, culturally through her Molière and Racine, France dominated the European stage for nearly two centuries. The Revolution of 1789 and the Napoleonic era stamped her as a first-class nation-state, which had already by the middle of the eighteenth century shot out long colonialist arms to Canada, India and the Far East and in the nineteenth century was making not unsuccessful passes at the African continent. The story of the French nation culminates in her bleeding during the First and Second World Wars, her retreat, though in quite a different style from the British from Empire, and her recent small-scale renaissance under General de Gaulle with his ambition to dominate the European community in such a way as to turn it into a "third force" in between the U.S.A. and the U.S.S.R. and regarding Britain as an unwelcome competitor for this role.

Algeria makes an absorbing topic for the study of an imperialist dependency turning into a nationally liberated independent state —particularly as this can illustrate another difference between the Latin and the Anglo-Saxon patterns of imperialism, namely the greater ease and readiness to cross "colour" bars—for example, the very coining of the cultural concept of "Négritude". Against the Berber background and the Arab conquest of the seventh century, the story of modern Algerian nationalism can be taken to begin with the challenge that promoted it in the French acquisition of Algeria in 1830. We notice next for our comparative purposes that by 1871 France had turned Algeria into three departments of metropolitan France and that European immigrants were already there. Then there developed the tension between those White French settlers and the government in Paris, which they considered as wrong in spending money on the education of native Moslems. Here we have a classic case for comparative treatment, notably in Rhodesia. Native nationalism began to stir after the First World War, first under Messali Hadj then under Ferhat Abbas (1942), Manifesto of the Algerian People claiming national independent sovereignty at the end of the war. In spite of the indignant opposition of the White settlers General de Gaulle allocated voting rights for the French Chamber in 1944 to the people over 21, a sign of his own realism and further evidence of the way in which national liberation movements could be influenced by their connection with events in the wider world scene. Compromise on these lines was, however, made impossible, and in March 1954 nine young Algerians formed the Revolutionary Council for Unity and Action. In spite of further attempts at settlement at Evian in 1962 further civil war ensued of a bitter and cruel kind not only between Europe and Algeria but between conflicting groups of the Algerians themselves. Once again the issue, noticed already in our comments on the Spanish–Mexican section, of national liberation and social reform, raised its head. "Independence is a stage: Revolution is an End." (A.L.N. notice.)

This part of the study can fittingly conclude with an analysis of the difference between Ben Bella and Ben-Khedda and an estimate the prospects of Colonel Boumédienne.

Sufficient hints, it is hoped, have now been given as to the potentialities for education for world understanding through this kind of systematic teaching of one kind of comparative nationalism: the European nationalist expansionist type with respective comebacks, but there are at least three other approaches which can be usefully adopted with the same end in view and which may therefore be properly considered here.

One is what might be described as the study of renovated nationalism. By this is meant the phenomenon of an ancient civilisation reappearing in the modern world in the garments of nationalism as defined at the beginning of this chapter. Four examples suggest themselves: Egypt, the origins of whose contemporary nationalism may be seen as the response to British control over that country in the second half of the nineteenth century and whose present prospects must be assessed in terms of the leadership of General Nasser; Israel, the origins of whose contemporary nationalism may be seen in the Balfour Declaration about a National Home for the Jews, and the championship of the Zionist cause by Chaim Weizman and whose present prospects must be assessed in terms of Israeli–Arab relations as a whole in the Middle East; India, the origins of whose contemporary nationalism may be seen as the response to British rule, the Congress Party's activities, Gandhi, Nehru and Independence and whose present prospects must be assessed in terms of her modernisation problems (Food and Industry and Population Control) and her external relations to Pakistan and China; Japan, the origins of whose contemporary nationalism may be seen as the imitative response to European imports to the Far East, the Russo-Japanese War, victory in the First World War and defeat in the Second, and whose present prospects must be assessed in terms of her experiment in mass technological democracy and her relations to the rest of the Asian world.

Equipped with the necessary minimum knowledge of the factual content of their origins and prospects, cross-references in these four cases could follow on a comparative studies basis and on the basis of a religious-philosophical and economic and a political theme. For example, the place of Coptic Christianity in Egypt, Judaism in Israel, Hinduism in India and Shintoism in Japan as being mutually contradictory or complementary in a total world setting of human beliefs: irrigation problems in Egypt and Israel, population control in India and Japan; types of political and social structures, Egypt and Pan-Arabism, Israel and Zionism, India's regionalisation and Japan's experiments in democratic government since the disappearance of Mikado rule. A further approach on comparative lines is indicated by the fact that in three cases the United Nations Organisation has been involved, more or less effectively, in some peace-keeping activity; the Suez affair in the case of Egypt, the Gaza strip in the case of Israel, Kashmir in the case of India. The key question then in this study of renovated nationalism is the degree to which modern nationalist quarrels have modified traditional social habits and tendencies and also the blend of them both most suitable to the history of an ordered world society.

Another method of proceeding, not altogether dissimilar from the above, would be to make a comparative study of ideological nationalism, and by this is meant the phenomena revealed by the U.S.A., the U.S.S.R. and China. With regard to the third we have an example of renovated nationalism, with regard to the second an example from Europe of an exported nationalism, and with regard to the first an example of isolationist nationalism, reacting against European exported nationalism, but itself a child of it and drawing its uniquely Americanised assimilated peoples from both West and East. In each case, moreover, nationalism sails under very clearly identifiable ideological colours, all stamped with the word "democracy" but this so variously interpreted as to mean freedom in one country and tyranny in another. Because these are the three giant nations of the modern world, they must form an essential ingredient in our exercise in comparative nationalism. Here therefore are a few suggestions for the purposes of comparative study:

1. The Genesis of American, Russian and Chinese Nationalism
   —A comparison of the 1776 Declaration of American Independence with the 1848 Communist Manifesto.
2. Biographical comparisons of
   Washington—Lenin—Sun Yat Sen,
   Jefferson—Trotsky—Chiang Kai chek,
   Lincoln—Stalin—Mao Tse tung.
3. A comparison of noted epics as ingredients of nationalism.
   The American "Frontier".
   The Modernisation of Siberia.
   The Great March.
4. A comparison of foreign policy since 1945 as a clue to the "Cold War".
5. If democracy can be defined as "government by public

opinion", how is it measured in the three nations covered and which by this standard measurement is the most or the least democratic?

Arising from considerations such as these is the crucial question, decisive really in education for world understanding, as to how far the very magnitudes themselves of the Great Powers in spite of or because of those differences in their ideological premise can act as stumbling-blocks or inducements to the evolution of world order, and at this stage there must be brought in a balanced appreciation of the military and economic capacity of each one of them.

Finally, there is the category, which may be labelled without any derogatory implication, of the pocket nationalisms. These have a particular importance within the context of our general theme, for they can provide evidence of the nationalist social impetus more easily observable small-scale model and at the same time afford striking testimony of ways in which they may contribute to the high drama of international relations. The three nation-states of Switzerland, Eire and Cuba suit our purpose admirably.

With regard to Switzerland the salient teaching features will be the historical antecedents of her "Neutrality" in modern history, how this has been a helpful contribution to the evolution of world institutions by the harbouring within her frontiers of the League of Nations, the International Labour Office and, since 1945, a whole host of governmental and non-governmental international agencies, and how even more recently traditional Swiss neutrality, while still preserved in many of its essentials, is having to yield ground to those global political and economic pressures, which make any real kind of "neutrality" among nations a highly dubious undertaking. Yet, and this is a sentence which may usefully be recorded for comparative use when considering our two other "pocket" nationalisms, "Not although she is neutral, but because she is neutral, Switzerland can render valuable services to an international peace organisation". (Bonjour, Offler and Potter, *A Short History of Switzerland*, p. 375, O.U.P., 1952.)

With regard to Eire, the origin of its nationalism can be presented as a long-delayed response to centuries of English overlordship culminating in the Easter Rising of 1916, Sinn Fein and eventual Independence under De Valera. By way of contrast with Switzerland there can be brought out here Ireland's failure to federate, i.e. Ulster as separate from Eire but by way of similarity Eire's contribution to the evolution of world institutions in the figure of Boland and the U.N. Headquarters in New York and Conor Cruse O'Brien's activities in the Congo. With regard to Cuba, the origin of its nationalism can be presented as a reaction against first Spanish and then U.S. imperialism, the second especially in economic terms, but its main significance will be as demonstrating how a national liberation movement under Fidel Castro becomes involved in a Great Power ideological struggle in the fateful encounter between Kruschev and Kennedy, when the fate of mankind seemed to turn on the issue of war and peace as between the U.S.S.R. and the U.S.A. over the matter of "missile" sites. Cuban nationalism as a thing in itself and Cuban nationalism as a pawn in power politics can lead on to a useful consideration of the different roles of pocket nationalisms, those which, as in the case of Cuba, lend themselves to the role of pawns (Albania would be another example), and those which do not (Finland would be another example here).

Enough material has been discussed to establish the contention that exercises in comparative nationalism are pedagogically useful in education for world understanding. The reasons for this may be briefly summarised. First, such an exercise can help to place "My Nation" in proper perspective, to whichever category it happens to belong. Secondly, it highlights what are the basic ingredients of the most potent socio-political force at present active in the world: these can be surveyed by laying alongside their various manifestations Rénan's definition of a nation made in 1882: "Avoir des gloires communes dans le passé, une volonté commune dans le présent, avoir fait de grandes choses ensemble, vouloir en faire encore; voilà les conditions essentielles pour être un peuple."

Thirdly, and especially by applying this Rénan yardstick, pupils can be brought to see that in many, though not in all, of the emerging nations the coming generation must learn to live realistically with the fact that there have been no common glories of the past which they can share. On the other hand, they do possess in massive measure a common will today, namely to achieve that material security and psychological self-realisation, both of which have previously been denied to all but a minority of the earth's inhabitants. For some again it will be proper to recall great memories of global deeds shared and also the possibility of repeating them, but only on such a sufficiently global scale as not to stultify them by a too parochial rehearsal of them. For, and this is where this particular series of lessons ends, the essential condition for being a people today is, in the words of the writer in the *Observer* newspaper (29 March 1964): ". . . to redeem the most spectacular failure in world politics in the past decade—the failure, in which America, Russia and Europe have all shared, of the new countries of the world to do anything effective to help the poorer ones to overcome their poverty." Education for world understanding should build substantially for that redemption.

CHAPTER 4

WORLD STUDIES

AT THE UNIVERSITY

By studying problems of world order university professors and students are reaffirming the perennial nature of their calling. At the dawn of their existence in mediæval Europe under theology, the queen of the sciences, scholarship was based on a cosmic premise which supported the various, specialist disciplines. Subsequently, and especially with the disappearance of that original Christian outlook, the universities not only in Europe but everywhere became more and more conglomerations of departmental specialisations.

With the Renaissance and Reformation came a shift in emphasis, from the theocentric to the anthropocentric, and the Industrial Revolution completed the process by means of which European society slipped the leashes of Christian faith and plunged confusedly into the pseudo-religions of uncurbed nationalism and production for gain as contrasted with production for use. The nature and significance of this essentially materialistic outlook of the nineteenth century were admirably summarised by Professor William McDougall:

> If materialism is true, human life, fundamentally and generally speaking, is not worth living; and men and women who believe materialism to be true will not in the long run think themselves justified in creating, in calling to life, new individuals to meet the inevitable pains and sorrows and labours of life and the risks of many things far worse than death. Human life, as we know it, is a tragic and pathetic affair which can only be redeemed by some belief or at least some hope in a larger significance than is compatible with the creed of materialism, no matter in how nobly stoic a form it may be held. A civilization which resigns itself wholly to materialism lives upon and consumes its moral capital and is incapable of renewing it.

How then does all this apply to the university? Until comparatively recent times the European universities created a barrier against the tendencies I have just outlined, and like all barriers this one had both a positive and negative aspect. On the credit side was the high standard of classical scholarship maintained in many universities, and before dismissing this wisdom of Greece and Rome too lightly let us recall Alexander Hamilton's description of the classical mind as one with "the capacity to see the essentials of any situation in great simplicity". Moreover, until the very end of the nineteenth century the universities provided a training-ground for responsible leaders, especially in the Civil Services and the professions, who possessed by implication if not by definition the ethical principles derived from their classical studies. On the debit side there were the increasingly sterile pedantry of professors and students and the perpetuation of university class privilege. It was this barrier which preserved the traditional university until the second decade of the present century and still made possible the maintenance among its members of a high standard of social morals and an almost hectic activity in scientific research.

Yet this barrier eventually proved ineffective in the face of two powerful forces, which were assailing it. The first of them was the rise of the pseudo-educated masses—those to whom the traditional university by its very own work had brought the opportunity for advancement. Large numbers of people, intoxicated with the heady wine of political emancipation and popular education recognised the weaknesses of the existing universities without understanding their strength: as Ortega y Gasset put it: "The characteristic of the hour is that the commonplace mind, knowing itself to be common place, has the assurance to proclaim the rights of the common place and to impose them wherever it will."

C. G. Jung has described at a deeper level still, how with the crumbling of the barrier the moral standards of society have experienced a landslide. "A man of today", he writes, "who corresponds more or less to the collective moral ideal, has made his heart into a den of murderers."

The second of these forces, a negative one also, was the increasingly glaring absence of any basic spiritual belief in society at large and in the university in particular. This was a state of affairs predicted nearly a hundred years earlier by Soren Kierkegaard, who as a young man was driven to that awe-inspiring confession, which many of us today can echo—"I stick my finger into existence: it smells of nothing." There seems to have been a threefold reaction in university circles to this predicament: the first was marked in England by the gloomy escapism of the poet-scholar A. E. Housman—neither the Shropshire Lad nor Juvenal could save him from a position essentially of despair. Then there was the attempt, often made in genuine good faith, of the scientists to elaborate a socially relevant theory of their science, which however tended to result in the prostitution of scientific truth to political expediency. Finally there was the tragic irrelevance of the Christian Church to the surging issues which swept into men's souls—an irrelevance which earned for the church from one of its more bitter critics a description as "the Fifth Column of Fate".

By the 1920's it was apparent that twin dangers menaced the European universities: one was their social irresponsibility, the other was a contrary and compensatory tendency to develop into appendages of the State. Retreat into an "ivory tower" though possible for a few, was nothing but a temporary and immoral palliative. The possible subservience of university to state, professor and student to politician and "big-business" became of furious concern in the field of research as for example in the use and abuse of nuclear physics. The university research worker of today is reluctant to submit his results to the state and yet owes a duty to the society of which he is a part and which he can generally only visualise in terms of his national unit. In the shadow of these dangers students became more and more mere products of an academic sausage-machine and universities mere technical schools for the fashioning of robots. Count Keyserling slyly pointed to another "escape" from the university dilemma as practised in the United States of America—the escape of athleticism: "An American university", he once remarked, "is an athletic association in which opportunities for study are provided for the feeble-bodied."

If there are some grains of truth in the kind of approach I have been suggesting, what we have been witnessing in Europe is the passing of a tradition from its mediaeval origin with a distinct metaphysical foundation to the idea of the liberal university, best summarised perhaps by the cry—"the pursuit of knowledge for its own sake". The events of the last thirty years have brought with them a series of challenges to this idea of the liberal university. One of these comes from Christianity itself. There are signs in this and other countries that a real attempt is being made to revive traditional Christian faith and doctrine in terms which the twentieth century can understand. However unsympathetic we may feel to church language and custom, we have to realise that here is a force, expressed not only by the old and decrepit but by some of the finest spirits of our age.

Another challenge is associated with pressure in the field of science and the tendency for universities to become entirely the mass-producers of technicians, who are masters of their technique but slaves of an out-of-date and immoral social system, both nationally and internationally considered. The third challenge came from the "isms", those expressions of the contemporary neurosis whether of the Right (Nazism and Fascism) or of the Left (Communism): they are the pressure of a political doctrine to compel the university into a new way of life. Indeed if we are to assess truly the function of the university, we must be prepared to see in these three totalitarianisms attempts at a cure of the social illness of our time. All neurosis, whether of the individual or group, is an attempt at cure, and it is therefore not surprising that we have experienced these neurotic symptoms at both the general and purely university levels.

Another challenge found expression among the students who took part in the various Resistance Movements of the Second World War: these young men and women repeatedly affirmed that they were not only fighting against the Nazis but that they were fighting for the establishment of a more just social order in which the university should have a clearly defined role to play.

What emerges therefore is that when applied to a section of society within an accepted *Weltanschauung* as in the Age of Faith or the hey-day of Liberalism, the function of the university was clear, namely to promote research to the glory of God and to train an administrative and cultural élite. The function of the university became confused when it had to be related to a wider social sphere—that is when it had to build a new relationship to the "emancipated peoples", who expressed themselves in Nationalist terms by mechanical methods without an accepted *Weltanschauung*. The real challenge therefore to the idea of the liberal university is a kind of intensified example of the general social problem of the twentieth century, namely how fragmentary, atomic man and society are to become whole—how in fact we can become holy people in an unwhole, power-politics driven, world, whole students in unholy universities. Slowly during the last thirty years, and nowhere more than in the universities, we have been becoming conscious of the meaning of our suffering, a process summed up in the remark: "I don't believe in God but I respond to him." This growing consciousness reveals that the critical problem in human relationships is that of trust: now the prototype of all trustful relations is the healthy parent–child, God–man relationship—a relationship which has been symbolised in different institutions at different times in history—the university was one of such institutions, which when functioning properly acted as the channel of trust between the most highly educated members of a civilisation. The problem of the function of the university today is therefore the problem of how to establish confidence between individuals and groups: how, to use Smuts' phrase, to recover "from a failure of nerve".

The function of the university of today and tomorrow is a fourfold one. First, its function is to enable the race of man to survive, for the university is where responsible feeling and thinking must be done regarding the use which man is going to make of his knowledge. We have to retap the spiritual springs of our being, which can alone reassert the primacy of spiritual and personal reality against that nihilism of perverted individualism which has found its suicidal climax in depersonalised collectivism and mass hysteria. Professors and students have to protest against the evils of the over-specialisation of knowledge: they must direct their research towards the synthesis of knowledge, towards wholeness of thinking and feeling in order that they themselves may become whole scholars and holy teachers of men.

The second function of the university is to defend itself from such external pressures, national or class, as could deflect it from performing its first function and to do so by itself constantly creating and influencing these pressures. In other words, it has to produce technicians, but they will only be "civilised technicians" if the universities which teach them their technique at the same time teach them to what end in life that technique should be applied.

The third function of the university is to create and maintain a power-house of world-loyalties, transcending political and economic ideologies by relating both to their psychological and spiritual origins.

The fourth function of the university is to relate all its teaching, arts and sciences, to the actual experience of the people who wield power in society. This is a tremendous educational experiment to see whether the great values of civilisation, previously the monopoly of the few, can be made accessible to the many without losing their basic quality in the process. There is a hidden element in the university, which would be lost if defined, and somehow it has got to be preserved in the wider social setting in which alone university studies can now be justified. John Middleton Murry in *The Free Society* once wrote: ". . . the individual person in the modern state is largely an illusion . . . he cannot *act* as an individual. In order that the individual may become integrated and real, he must will acts which are within the range of possible action by society as a whole."

That judgement applies with equal force to the university: to be effective, it must "will acts which are within the range of possible action by the society as a whole".

It is against the background of some such assessment of the evolution of university tradition that the contemporary tasks of universities throughout the world begin to become clear: they have to bring their specialist studies increasingly to bear on those problems of world order, which require the most exact attentions of scholarship on an interdisciplinary basis. The harbingers of this development were the departments of International Relations as well as the ever-increasing number of learned societies which found it necessary more and more to operate on a global scale. The Institute of Intellectual Co-operative of the League of Nations, UNESCO and the International Association of University Teachers have been further signs of the times. As Professor Goodwin of the London School of Economics and Politics, of the University of London says:

> With this powerful ally (international history) on its flank international relations then consists of three main points. The first consists of a study of the International Political system, of the emergence and growth of the system of sovereign states (from about the 16th century to the present) and of the political processes at work within it. The second, Foreign Policy Analysis, is concerned with how foreign policy is made and executed, with the chance to specialise on the foreign policy of either the U.K., the U.S.A. or the Soviet Union. The third, International Institution, identifies and analyses the roles (diplomatic and legal) of international society and assesses their contributions, and that of international organisations (such as the League of Nations, the United Nations, the World Bank, NATO, the European Community, the International Communist Movement) to the maintaining and strengthening of world order. (*World Studies Education Service Bulletin* No. 2, Jan. 1967.)

What we are now witnessing is a transition to the next phase, when International Relations, from having been one among a number of other university disciplines, force all those subjects to contribute their expertise on an interdisciplinary basis to the study and solution of the problem of world order. These will still include for a while the relation between nation-states but will go far beyond that in order to cope with such topics as world law, world currencies, world communications.

In his Introduction to *Problems of World Order* (Report on the Isle of Thorns Summer School, 12–21 August 1966) H. L. Elvin,

Director of the London University Institute of Education, defined the character of this tendency:

> By a world order we mean simply the establishment of institutions and the working out of procedures and the growth of attitudes of mind that, for purposes where no smaller social unit will serve our interests now, have mankind as a whole for their constituency.
>
> We observed that in many studeis such developments had begun to take place, both in the teaching of undergraduates and in post-graduate study and research. International and comparative law were not very new subjects and the emerging law of nations was not regarded as unsuitable for study. International trade had long engaged the attention of economists. Now international economic institutions and economic aid organised through world institutions had a degree of attention. Social development, in terms both of general similarity and of local diversity, was equally an increasing subject of research. And in educational studies, both of policy and of school and university practice, a world view was becoming increasingly common.
>
> What is being done in universities and other institutions of higher education to study these changing conditions of life, and their consequences, for mankind?
>
> We made such enquiries as we could, and we did gather some information. But in truth this is a field in which only an officially sponsored inquiry, by, for instance, an "ad hoc" committee of the University Grants Committee, could do the job properly. It was indeed our hope that a survey of this kind would be the first action taken, since logically it is the first. And we felt that it might well lead to a special encouragement of this broad field of developing, but inadequately developed, studies such as has happened through U.G.C. initiative.
>
> That less is being done at present than needs to be done is a fair assumption. There have been individual studies of some importance, such as the late Dr. Loveday's study of the administrative problems of international organisations and Professor Arthur Lewis' internationally minded Theory of Economic Development and Dr. Robert Gardiner's Reith Lectures on the problems of race. There have been interesting ventures in teaching, both as developments of existing disciplines and in world affairs "as such". But when we think of the need for concentrated, high-level work of an inter-disciplinary kind, uniting the efforts of the political theorist, the expert on government, the economist, the sociologist, the planner, the technologist, and the educationist, can we say we are content? I meet rather frequently young people who ardently desire a career in international organisations, or on the international side of some established career, and they ask where they can get the proper training. At present, in this country, it is extremely difficult to say with confidence what the answer is.
>
> Where is the conceptual framework for such a further education and training? It seemed to us that major contributions must be made from within established disciplines. The person who presumes to advise on the

problems of a world economy must first be a good economist, the educational adviser a man well grounded not only in educational theory in general, but in comparative education; and so on. But almost every piece of serious world-wide planning and development, and of national development with outside aid, requires a collaboration between these different fields of expertise. This must be prepared for in study and in the training we give. Then, again, is not the word "international" too ambiguous and inappropriate for what we now have in mind? We do not mean simply, "between nations". We are thinking of institutions and procedures that are not merely between, say, two nations, but world-wide in their scope. Where, if not in institutions of higher learning and education, should such concepts be analysed, tested and refined—and brought to bear?

If the answer to that question is, as it surely must be, "in the world's universities", we should make some attempt to formulate one or two proposals by way of suggestive examples.

At the first degree level might it not be realistic and helpful to require every student of whatever faculty to prepare a short thesis as part of his degree course on the contribution of his particular specialism, be it Botany or Psychology or Statistics, to the building of world order. For example, a young woman studying Engineering in Israel might write on the application of Hydraulics to dam-building in the developing countries, or a young man studying History in Dublin might write on the significance of Minority Rights in contemporary world affairs. Alternatively each student could be required as part of his final first degree examination in whatever subject to answer three questions in a paper on Contemporary World Studies, samples of which might be:

1. Give an account of the peace-keeping machinery of the United Nations Organisation.
2. Comment on the causes of racial tension in any one region of the world.
3. Describe the contribution of one of the following to the building of a world society: (a) Hammarskjöld, (b) Nansen, (c) Danilo Dolci.

In addition to the above kind of elementary basic training for all kinds of University students, there would need to be undertaken more detailed and sustained work at the postgraduate and research level. Here there are a number of promising developments, three of which can be mentioned in passing. One is the work of the Conflict Research Centre at Michigan University, Ann Arbor: another is the Centre for Research in Collective Psychopathology at the University of Sussex, and a third is the pioneering effort of the World Law Fund of the U.S.A. Under its aegis there have appeared four volumes with the general title of *The Strategy of World Order*, edited by Richard A. Falk and Saul H. Mendlovitz, Volume I being *Toward a Theory of War Prevention*, Volume II *International Law*, Volume III *The United Nations*, Volume IV *Disarmament and Economic Development*.

As Harold D. Lasswell remarks in his foreword to the first volume: "The idea that serious intellectual effort can play an important role in achieving a positive resolution of the dilemmas of the age is a declaration of confidence in the human mind. . . . The proposed disciplinary concentration on world order is congenial to the future-orientated outlook of modern man" (p. iii–iv). That kind of "confidence in the human mind" is illustrated by the way in which these four volumes provide documentary evidence regarding one of the models for attaining a peaceful world order, namely *World Peace Through World Law* by Grenville Clark and Louis B. Sohn (Harvard U.P., 1964), an ingenious blueprint for a limited world government. Useful though that exercise has been, it has suffered from the defect that it must be regarded as based on a fantastic assumption, namely that as Richard Falk expresses it (*Saturday Review*, 21 May 1966):

> Such a peace plan was actually among the political choices open to statesmen. (Frederick the Great expressed his reaction to the Abbe St. Pierre's plan for World Peace in a letter to Voltaire: "The thing is most practicable; for its success all that is lacking is the consent of Europe and a few other trifles.") . . . The new style of education in war–peace problems is very sensitive to the defects of these earlier attempts to promote the reform of international society. Great attention is now given to a systematic study of the period of transition between one international system and another. . . . Some understanding is sought of why it is so difficult to change the structure of international society in an interwar period, of why the inertia of the political bureaucracy in large states is so great that no change of any significance seems likely to become politically feasible. . . .

> The educational task is usually conceived as a double one. First, the possibilities of reform within the existing international system are examined. Such an outlook is essentially conservative and devoted to system-maintenance, i.e. The Limited Nuclear Test Ban, the United Nation Resolution prohibiting the deployment of weapons of mass destruction in outer space, the "hot-line", and electronic locks to prevent unauthorised use of nuclear weapons. The second appraisal examines the possibilities of transforming the existing international system. . . . In this more radical context of system-change, the educated effort is primarily to imagine coherent models of world order and to study transition strategies for bringing them into being.

One such feat of imagination is contained in a publication by the Carnegie Endowment for International Peace on International Conciliation, entitled *The Political Equivalent of War—Civilian Defense* by Gene Sharp (November 1965, No. 555). As the Editor in Chief says in his Preface:

> Alternatives to war have long exercised the minds of men, but there has been little effort to build upon the foundation of experience. One area of such experience is nonviolent response to aggression and tyranny. Sporadically, more or less successfully, more or less importantly, citizens have for centuries sought through boycotts, passive resistance, strikes, and non-cooperation to oppose the armed power of authority, be it that of an aggressor or of a totalitarian regime.
>
> The present article is one of the early contributions to the effort to order this material and appraise the implications, potentialities, and limitations of "civilian defense" (using the technique of nonviolent action) as a viable alternative to war. It raises more questions than it answers and, undoubtedly, still more remain imbedded in the unexplored matrix of experience and political realities. But, as Alastair Buchan, the Director of the Institute for Strategic Studies, has pointed out, the fact that "the older defensive strategies have become totally outmoded by technical innovations" requires "increasing attention to the indirect strategies for preserving our societies from domination of external rule". It may be that "in concepts like the nonviolent defence of countries lies the key to the preservation of society".

Another feat would be to organise the systematic preparation of case-histories in connection with recent crises in world affairs. A start in this direction has been made with the World Studies Reader, which seeks to apply the following hypothesis, namely that a capacity to analyse public controversy is an essential part of training for world citizenship, to the Congo, Rhodesia, Suez, the Nuremburg Trial, Vietnam and other subjects. (For details, apply

World Law Fund, 11 West 42nd Street, New York.) Closely aligned to that kind of enterprise is the encouragement in universities of the study of documents: here we have a model in *The World Studies Series* (Routledge & Kegan Paul), volumes on Malaysia and her Neighbours, The European Community and the Kennedy regime are already published and others on India–Pakistan, Brazil, Apartheid, The Middle East, Soviet Foreign Policy, U.N. Peace-Keeping Machinery, Pan-Africanism and Political Parties in twentieth-century China are already in preparation.

From even such brief considerations as the above, it is clear that universities today are on the brink of rediscovering and restating their unique function, namely to make scholarly sense of the human scene in its entirety.

B. FURTHER AND ADULT EDUCATION

Under both of these headings we have now to return to the challenging problem referred to in Chapter 3, namely, what can be done in the way of education for world understanding for that majority of the human race that leaves school at 14 or 15 or even earlier? We shall distinguish here between them (Further Education) and those who may have had a fuller or different kind of education up to 18 or 19 but who in their 30's, 40's and later demand cultural sustenance in these matters (Adult Education).

1. *Further Education*

For these older adolescents the young men and women comprising the vast majority of humanity, education for world understanding has to overcome three difficulties: first, that most of its pupils are unapproachable through the printed word except in its briefest and most direct form; secondly, that the occasions on which any educational activity is possible will tend to be non-continuous, spasmodic, inconsistent; thirdly, that because of unfortunate experiences of learning while in school many of these junior citizens of one world will have developed a resistance against learning anything. Yet it is precisely this category of human beings who will vote and trade and play and decide by their more or less conscious attitudes the issue between genocide and survival of the species.

What dare we then propose?

First, that what is immediately relevant to them, their local way of life, be shown to them as only making sense in the greater context of global relevance.

Secondly, that this demonstration be achieved by providing them constantly and consistently with experiences of meeting their contemporaries on common ground, the nature of which they can test out for themselves.

Thirdly, that this common ground should consist (a) of actual personal meeting by means of work and holiday exchanges and where that is not possible by means of vicarious meeting through the medium of television and the medium of video-tapes; (b) shared professional interests, e.g. young telephonists of the world unite; (c) shared aesthetic and athletic experiences, e.g. dancing and making music and outward bound groups; (d) sharing a common knowledge of world events by all the possible means of mass communication.

Let us try and attach some concrete suggestions to each of these proposals in turn. With regard to local way of life and global relevance we might take the following two cases. First, a young man serving his apprenticeship as a fisherman from one of the Pacific coastal ports: he sees the amount of his boat's daily or weekly "catch", what happens to it, how much money he and his more experienced fishermen get into their own pockets from its sale, why this seems to vary according to fluctuation in the market prices, what are the causes of this fluctuation. . . . So he can be led on to an interest in the lives and earnings of fellow-fishermen in other seas than his and why they earn more or less than he does: then, what proportion of food consumption is made up of fish consumption in different societies and, finally and above all, how can the total world production of fish for food be increased by the scientific harvesting of the oceans? Secondly, a young girl in her first office job as a junior typist in Tokyo or New York: what is her daily routine, how is she employed, what skills has she at her command, how far is she nothing but a tiny cog in a vast machine, what chances are there for her to "better" herself by becoming maybe the boss's private secretary; on what do prospects of promotion depend? This can then be taken further with guesses as to the probable supercession of human clerical assistants by machines and the implication of this for her and the thousands of other juniors like her, and further still how the activities of the particular office in which she works connect with the great global problems of politics, economics and culture. Enough has been hinted at to make the point that each individual can be shown that his own little activity is taking place in a world, which however mad it seems, is in fact merely growing.

With regard to the second of our proposals, and here we link up with the idea of adventure for peace referred to in Chapter 2, a wide range of voluntary organisation as well as governmental agencies are available, for example the Central Bureau for Educational Visits, Exchanges and Voluntary Service Overseas: the main difficulty here is to ensure that such facilities are known about and that many more young people than at present be encouraged to make use of them. Even when actual exchanges or visits are not possible, much can be achieved by means of such schemes as pen-friends, exchange of special youth television programmes and travelling exhibitions.

Another line of approach is via professional interests: let there be regular meetings of young workers, skilled, semi-skilled and unskilled, where the common problems they are involved in when earning their livelihood can be discussed and perhaps solved. For example, young radio engineers employed in aircraft production compare their conditions of work, aviation technicalities, similarities and differences in equipment; or young farmers confer about the use of artificial insemination in stock-rearing in different parts of the world; or public-transport workers consult on the best means for securing smooth collaboration from their various publics.

Sport of all kinds, provided it can steer clear of racism, supplies another ready and congenial channel of communication: playing with one another is being most truly ourselves and therefore most truly meeting one another: the touring football team at however modest a level of proficiency can achieve more than a trainload of mere supporting "fans", though these are not to be despised. Then for many more young men and women than might be supposed, joint pursuits in the arts and crafts make admirable occasions for friendly collaboration. Here there spring to mind three examples: meetings of young artists at the Museum of Modern Art in Frankfurt-am-Main, Germany; International Voluntary Service work camps whose housing projects are undertaken in necessitous areas; and thirdly, quite spontaneous and individual efforts such as that of two young carpenters who are on permanent trek round the world, living off their handicraft skill and penetrating thoroughly into a whole host of different cultures: straight sawing is welcome behind all ideological curtains!

Finally, if public opinion about the problems of world order is to gain steadily in wisdom and influence, ways must be found of informing all those millions of young folk about what is going on. News is, however, so easily and even deliberately distorted that many young people react violently to it in one of two ways: either they say "It's in the paper; therefore it must be true" or "You can never trust the papers". Possibly what is needed therefore is a kind of special "Peace-keeping Journalist branch of United Nations Organisation", specially charged with interpreting current events, political, economic and cultural, in such a way as to demonstrate that the whole gigantic panorama of world affairs is not just a nonsense, that the non-sense it often does appear to make, when, for example, societies prefer guns to butter, can make perfectly good sense when referred to those constants of judgement suggested earlier in this book as being essential for the right ordering of the world's activities. The executive of this United Nations Organisation board would operate from a common base by means of the best mass media of instruction, and they would be the paid officials of the United Nations Organisation.

2. *Adult Education*

Here we may assume in the first place that adult education programmes, if sufficiently attractively advertised and efficiently staffed, can be aimed at willing and attentive students. True that most of them will only be able to give part of their time to their study, possibly at the end of a fatiguing day's work and also that many of them will have had a stunted or unsuccessful school career behind them, but they possess two great advantages: first they themselves genuinely desire to find out and learn, and secondly they bring to their reading and writing a diverse wealth of experience in the ways of the world. In studying problems of world order, this last consideration can be of immense value.

In addition to the numerous courses already being run in History, International Affairs, Sociology and so on, every adult education teaching unit, it may be suggested, could undertake simultaneously on-going programmes of work in all quarters of the globe with one central theme, namely "Spanning the gap between present international disorder and future global order—how to make the transition." This would mean a careful and systematic untying of the three great thorny knots, which at present hinder such an evolution. The fact that students in adult education classes everywhere were engaged in this common activity and knew that they were so engaged, and that they corresponded with one another about it and visited each other in connection with it, could in itself forge another mighty bond of understanding among embryo world citizens. Let us finger each of these knots in turn and see what kind of syllabus content they might suggest for an adult education class in city and countryside.

Politically, the knot is constituted by the problems involved in passing from a state of affairs where final, absolute sovereignty is vested in the nation-state to a situation in which a sufficient degree of national political sovereignty has been surrendered for a supranational legislative and executive and judiciary to function effectively in matters over which nations no longer have the capacity to decide autonomously. The obvious example here is arms control, and this would involve an examination of the causes and course of the League of Nations, and the United Nations Organisation, together with an assessment of how the latter needs to be reformed or replaced if some kind of organ of world government is to emerge.

Economically, the knot is constituted by the world's food and population problem, and a wonderful study topic immediately suggests itself, namely how are India and China coping or failing to cope with the colossal task of feeding their increasing millions. The kind of material such an adult education class would handle is dramatically suggested in a talk by Max Kirschner, printed in *The Listener* of 26 January 1967, and entitled "Wilful Waste, Woeful Want: India's Agriculture".

> Hunger causes internal insecurity and often uncertainty of political attitude which has an estranging effect on the "White" and the "Red" world from which all help must come. These twenty years of development aid have established a partition in three groups. The White or capitalistic world and the Red one—between themselves one-third of mankind—are defined by their economic systems and their political outlook just as the Third World is marked by the absence of any common system and the prevalence of emotions like distrust, anger and despair. Violent feelings and the common danger of the approaching catastrophe are the seeds of the Third World: a catastrophe which will make some of the Third World countries uninhabitable places within thirty years—and some within ten.

Mr. Kirschner then goes on to point out the stark implications of this in India itself:

> Most of the reasons of Indian misery can be compressed into one sentence: the people are still waging a suicidal war against the agricultural basis of their own existence. They waste primary natural resources on a scale that no other nation does. . . . Thus they stack away 410 million tons of dung a year. Another 600 million tons get lost in grazing areas, and only 215 million tons are actually used for manuring Indian fields.

As is said in Henderson and Caldwell's *The Chainless Mind* Hamish Hamilton, 1967):

> The contrast with China could hardly be more complete. The present upheaval connected with the proletarian cultural revolution cannot obscure the underlying economic success of the regime since 1949. Mistakes have been made, but overall progress has also been made.

> Western observers returning from China, however adverse their comments on the consequences of the cultural revolution, agree that the food shops mirror a country which is no longer hungry and the streets a people no longer poor in the sense of the age-old poverty of Asia.

Here then is a tough knot for the teacher and his class to untie—the reasons for this difference, the influence of climate and beliefs, the relevance of India's and China's exposure to other parts of the Third World.

Psychologically, the knot is constituted by the inadequately broad span of human awareness and sympathy. This means that the adult education class should pay attention to the ways in which the spans of individual and group consciousness do in fact expand (see Introduction), how the extent of social loyalties can be stretched. They will take into account what is known of the mechanisms of "In" and "Out" group behaviour and familiarise themselves with the kind of information contained in such a book as Durbin and Bowlby's *Personal Aggressiveness and War* (Kegan Paul, 1938). They will be required to ponder such a sentence as the following: "Possessiveness, frustration, animism are potent causes of conflict between groups—whether parties, classes or states. . . . It seems probable that the complex character of the civilised individual undergoes a degeneration or simplification into simpler forms and simpler reactions when he is caught up into and expresses himself through the unity of the group" (p. 15). By these and other means a tutor and his class can come to the fundamental question as to what it is that is the ultimate fact between human beings, that which lies beyond the shared interests of body and mind, that element which is so highly esteemed that men and women are known to sacrifice gladly their own lives in its service—what in short makes it possible for men to trust their neighbour when any "realistic" interpretation of history proves him untrustworthy?

The posing of such a question suggests another extremely fruitful method of approaching world affairs in adult education, namely by the use of the novel. For "it is through the novelist's power of creation that we can get our best glimpse of what lies behind the reverberatory power of facts" (Marcel, *The Mystery of Being*). As has been said of Tolstoy's *War and Peace*, "Life would speak thus if life could speak". Fiction, as E. M. Forster points out in his *Aspects of the Novel* (p. 10), occupies that "spongy tract of land", which lies between poetry and history, and adds: "If God could tell the story of the universe, the Universe would become fictitious" (p. 55). Let us try out this proposition for ourselves by taking a few novels and seeing just how they can be made use of for our pedagogical purpose. However severely tempted the teacher may be to select a book because of its obvious and immediate relevance to some current or real international crisis, such as the Algerian and Congo situations so excitingly handled by David Caute in *The Decline of the West*, he must resist this temptation in the interests of real literary quality and merit, because, after all, the students will be trafficking with the text of any work for quite a time and so it must wear well. It is assumed that all the members of an adult education class will have prepared for the following studies by making a preliminary reading of the texts of each novel.

A start could be made by using Robert Musil's *The Man Without Quality* as an exploratory way in to the nature of the twentieth century, what it is all about, seen chiefly in the predicament of European man. Set in the Vienna of 1913 this long novel, written by Musil over the period 1930–52, is both the analysis of a spent society, "Kakania" and an uncannily prophetic comment on the advent of various forms of totalitarianisms. In individual, as distinct from collective terms, it is concerned with modern man's alienation in the figure of Ulrich, the "man without qualities", because that which goes to put a man together, to make a whole of him, is lacking and therefore the separate qualities have no point of focus in him. The following passage might well form the first text for discussion by the class:

> In earlier times one could be an individual with a better conscience than one can to-day. People used to be like the stalks of corn in a field. They were probably more violently flung to and fro by God, hail, fire, pestilence and war than they are to-day, but it was collectively, in terms of towns, of countrysides, the field as a whole; and whatever was left to the individual stalk in the way of personal movement was something that

could be answered for and was clearly defined. To-day, on the other hand, responsibility's point of gravity lies not in the individual but in the relations between things. Has one not noticed that experiences have made themselves independent of man? Who to-day can still say that his anger is really his own anger, with so many people butting in and knowing so much more about it than he does? There has arisen a world of qualities without a man to them, of experiences without anyone to experience them, and it almost looks as though under ideal conditions man will no longer experience anything at all privately and the comforting weight of personal responsibility would dissolve into a system of formulae for potential meanings. It is probable that the dissolution of the anthropocentric attitude (an attitude that after so long seeing man as the centre of the universe, has been dissolving for some centuries now) has finally began to affect the personality itself; for the belief that the most important thing about experience is the experiencing of it, and about deeds the doing of them, is beginning to strike most people as naive. (Vol. I, pp. 174–5.)

Several pedagogical exercises spring to mind. (1) Find examples of the protest of individual conscience in different twentieth-century societies. (2) What evidence is there for the progressive atomisation of man in his work and leisure in twentieth-century society? (3) In what ways have the various twentieth-century isms taken the place of the traditional religions? Then the students could be asked to consider the following, quoted by Barton Pike in *Robert Musil: An Introduction to His Work* (Cornell U.P., 1961, p. 125):

Malcolm Cowley, writing in The Literary Situation about the "new" American writers of the 1950's has expressed it (the predicament of the "Man Without Quality") typically:

"I think the real background of this work is a sort of horror at what is happening in the world—not a specialised horror at any one development like atomic weapons, totalitarian governments, the cold war, or the restriction on personal liberty in all countries, but rather a generalised dismay at the results of five centuries of progress and widening enlightenment. Men have outrun themselves, their technical knowledge has increased so much more rapidly than their moral judgment and self control and simple kindness—if these have increased at all—that the knowledge might destroy them as a species. . . . Combined with the fear of catastrophe is the feeling that individuals are unable to prevent it."

How do the characters in Musil's three volumes illustrate this contention? "There is no longer a whole man confronting a whole world, but a human something floating about in a universal culture-medium." (Vol. I, p. 257.)

The characters of Arnheim (based on that of Rathenau) and Moosbrugger, the great criminal, can in themselves lead into an understanding of how power and spirit have become alienated from one another in our times and how, not far beneath the level of consciousness, there lurks in each one of us the "Moosbrugger" shadow side of human personality, capable of appalling crimes and inhumanity—the clue to the concentration-camp phenomena. Above all Musil's depicting of the contemporary human scene as a kind of climax can be noted—the climax of anarchy as an expression of the clash between a false, sentimental internationalism (the "Do-gooders") and fanatic chauvinism (the "dare men"), together with one of Musil's rare suggestions for remedy: "In sum the function of the novel is to recognise and present the 'good evil' because that is what the world needs more than a utopian 'goody-good' " (p. 1635).

A second novel might be either Thomas Mann's *The Magic Mountain* or *Dr. Faustus*: let us glance at the possibilities of the latter. It is an introduction to the daemonic in modern life, exemplified in the figure of Adrian Leverkuhn—the modern Faust. The story is told by his friend, who is actually writing it in the closing stages of the Second World War when the Hitler fortress is beginning to crumble under Allied bombardment and invasion. Several passages could be selected to demonstrate how the Nazi phenomenon was a specially odious instance of a generally prevailing contemporary disease—that of the disorientated complex urban heaps of industrialised and frustrated men and woman. One passage must suffice here, taken from a closing chapter of Mann's great morality:

> Since the end of March—it is now the 25th of April in this year of destiny 1945—our resistance in the west has been visibly disintegrating. The papers, already half-unmuzzled, register the truth. Rumour, fed by enemy announcements on the radio and stories told by fugitives, knows no censorship, but carries the individual details of swiftly spreading catastrophe about the land, into regions not yet swallowed, not yet liberated by it, and even hither into my retreat. No hold any more: everybody surrenders, everybody runs away. Our shattered, battered cities fall like ripe plums. Darmstadt, Wurzburg, Frankfurt are gone; Mannheim and Cassell, even Münster and Leipzig are in foreign hands. One day the

English reached Bremen, the Americans were at the gates of Upper Franconia; Nuremberg, city of the national celebrations so uplifting to unenlightened hearts, Nuremberg surrendered. The great ones of the regime, who wallowed in power, riches, and wrong, now rage and kill themselves: justice is done.

Russian corps after taking Könisberg and Vienna were free to force the Oder; they moved a million strong against the capital, lying in its rubble, already abandoned by all the government officials. Russian troops carried out with their heavy artillery the sentence long since inflicted from the air. They are now approaching the centre of Berlin. Last year the horrible man escaped with his life—by now surely only an insanely flaring and flickering existence—from the plot of desperate patriots trying to salvage the future of Germany and the last remnant of her material goods. Now he has commanded his soldiery to drown in a sea of blood the attack on Berlin and to shoot every officer who speaks of surrender. And the order has been in considerable measure obeyed. At the same time strange radio messages in German, no longer quite sane, rove the upper air; some of them commend the population to the benevolence of the conquerors, even including the secret police, who they say have been much slandered. Others are transmitted by a "freedom movement" christened Werwolf: a band of raving-mad lads who hide in the woods and break out nightly; they have already deserved well of the Fatherland by many a gallant murder of the invaders. The fantastic mingles with the horrible: up to the very end the crudely legendary, the grim deposit of saga in the soul of the nation, is invoked, with all its familiar echoes and reverberations.

A transatlantic general has forced the population of Weimar to file past the crematories of the neighbouring concentration-camp. He declared that these citizens—who had gone in apparent righteousness about their daily concerns and sought to know nothing, although the wind brought to their noses the stench of burning human flesh—he declared that they too were guilty of the abominations on which he forced them now to turn their eyes. Was that unjust? Let them look, I look with them. In spirit I let myself be shouldered in their dazed or shuddering ranks. Germany had become a thick-walled underground torture-chamber, converted into one by a profligate dictatorship vowed to nihilism from its beginnings on. Now the torture-chamber has been broken open, open lies our shame before the eyes of the world. Foreign commissions inspect those incredible photographs everywhere displayed, and tell their countrymen that what they have seen surpasses in horribleness anything the human imagination can conceive. I say our shame. For is it mere hypochondria to say to oneself that everything German, even the German mind and spirit, German thought, the German Word, is involved in this scandalous exposure and made subject to the same distrust? Is the sense of guilt quite morbid which makes one ask oneself the question how Germany, whatever her future manifestations, can ever presume to open her mouth in human affairs?

Let us call them the sinister possibilities of human nature in general that here come to light. German human beings, tens of thousands, hundreds of thousands of them it is, who have perpetrated what humanity shudders at; and all that is German now stands forth as an abomination and a warning. How will it be to belong to a land whose history witnesses this hideous default; a land self-maddened, psychologically burnt-out, which quite understandably despairs of governing itself and thinks it for the best that it become a colony of foreign powers; a nation that will have to live shut in like the ghetto Jews, because a frightfully swollen hatred round all its borders will not permit it to emerge; a nation that cannot show its face outside?

Curses, curses on the corrupters of an originally decent species of human being, law-abiding, only too docile, only all too willingly living on theory, who thus went to school to Evil! How good it is to curse—or rather how good it would be, if only the cursing came from a free and unobstructed heart! We are present at the last gasp of a blood state which, as Luther put it, "took on its shoulders" immeasurable crimes; which roared and bellowed to the ravished and reeling masses proclamations cancelling all human rights; which set up its gaudy banners for youth to march under, and they marched, with proud tread and flashing eyes, in pure and ardent faith. But a patriotism which would assert that a blood state like that was so forced, so foreign to our national character that it could not take root among us: such a patriotism would seem to me more high-minded than realistic. For was this government, in word and deed, anything but the distorted, vulgarised, besmirched symbol of a state of mind, a notion of world affairs which we must recognise as both genuine and characteristic? Indeed, must not the Christian and humane man shrink as he sees it stamped upon the features of our greatest, the mightiest embodiments of our essential Germanness? I ask—and should I not? Ah, it is no longer in question that this beaten people now standing wild-eyed in face of the void stand there just because they have failed, failed horribly in their last and uttermost attempt to find the political form suited to their particular needs. (pp. 480-2.)

A third novel, which chooses itself, is Boris Pasternak's *Dr. Zhivago*, both for its sweeping survey of the ideological and human impacts of the Russian Revolution on Russia and others and also for the light it throws once again on the plight of the individual conscience imprisoned in totalitarian conditions as instanced in the censorship of Pasternak's novel in the U.S.S.R. Students in an adult education class can be brought to stare steadily and unafraid into the mystery of history itself. "History is not made by anyone. You cannot make history, nor can you see history, any more than you can watch the grass growing. Wars and revolutions, kings and Robespierres, are history's organic agents, its yeast" (p. 406).

Let them consider Fidel Castro, Mao Tse tung, Nyerere as "history's organic agents", let them compare on the grand scale, imaginatively conceived by Pasternak for his hero, Jury, the wars and revolutions of other continents.

A fourth novel could be Albert Camus' *The Fall*, with its penetrating study of the "Judge-Penitent"—still yet another variation of the predicament of "modern man in search of a soul".

"Fancy the Cro-Magnoñ man lodged in the Tower of Babel!" This pithy statement of man's dilemma comes in the opening sentences of Camus' tale: "I sometimes think of what future historians will say of us. A single sentence will suffice for modern man: he fornicated and read the papers" (p. 254).

Exercise for the students: How far is this an accurate summing up of Europe's drift to Munich? Or they might be asked to analyse one of the great power-struggles of the twentieth century, say on the Israeli–Arab frontiers or round the periphery of South Africa in the light of the following passage:

> Power, on the other hand, settles everything. It took time, but we finally realised that. For instance, you must have noticed that even old Europe at last philosophises in the right way. We no longer say as in simple times: "This is my opinion. What are your objections? We have become lucid. For the dialogues, we have substituted the communique."
> "This is the truth, we say. You can discuss it as much as you want: we aren't interested. But in a few years' time there'll be the police to show you I'm right." (p. 268.)

Finally, to illustrate a twentieth-century imperialist and racial problem, E. M. Forster's great novel *A Passage to India* could be chosen. Here are some general references: "They (Indians) were discussing as to whether or not it is possible to be friends with an Englishman" (p. 8), or the final pages in that most poignant dialogue between Aziz and Fielding:

> Aziz grew more excited. He rose in his stirrups and pulled at his horse's head in the hope it would rear. Then he should feel in a battle. He cried: "Clear out, all you Turtons and Burtons. We wanted to know you ten years back—now it's too late. If we see you and sit on your committees, it's for political reasons, don't you make any mistake." His horse did rear. "Clear out, clear out, I say. Why are we put to so much suffering? We used to blame you, now we blame ourselves, we grow wiser. Until

England is in difficulties we keep silent, but in the next European war—aha, aha! Then is our time." He paused, and the scenery, though it smiled, fell like a gravestone on any human hope. They cantered past a temple to Hanuman—God so loved the world that he took monkey's flesh upon him—and past a Saivite temple, which invited to lust, but under the semblance of eternity, its obscenities bearing no relation to those of our flesh and blood. They splashed through butterflies and frogs; great trees with leaves like plates rose among the brushwood. The divisions of daily life were returning, the shrine had almost shut.

"Who do you want instead of the English? The Japanese?" jeered Fielding, drawing rein.

"No, the Afghans. My own ancestors."

"Oh, your Hindu friends will like that, won't they?"

"It will be arranged—a conference of Oriental statesmen."

"It will indeed be arranged."

"Old story of 'We will rob every man and rape every woman from Peshawar to Calcutta,' I suppose, which you get some nobody to repeat and then quote every week in the *Pioneer* in order to frighten us into retaining you! We know!" Still he couldn't quite fit in Afghans at Mau, and, finding he was in a corner, made his horse rear again until he remembered that he had or ought to have, a mother-land. Then he shouted: "India shall be a nation! No foreigners of any sort! Hindu and Moslem and Sikh and all shall be one! Hurrah! Hurrah for India! Hurrah! Hurrah!"

India a nation! What an apotheosis! Last comer to the drab nineteenth-century sisterhood! Waddling in at this hour of the world to take her seat! She, whose only peer was the Holy Roman Empire, she shall rank with Guatemala and Belgium perhaps! Fielding mocked again. And Aziz in an awful rage danced this way and that, not knowing what to do, and cried: "Down with the English anyhow. That's certain. Clear out, you fellows, double quick, I say. We may hate one another, but we hate you most. If I don't make you go, Ahmed will, Karim will, if it's fifty five-hundred years we shall get rid of you, yes, we shall drive every blasted Englishman into the sea, and then"—he rode against him furiously—"and then," he concluded, half kissing him, "you and I shall be friends".

"Why can't we be friends now?" said the other, holding him affectionately. "It's what I want. It's what you want."

But the horses didn't want it—they swerved apart; the earth didn't want it, sending up rocks through which riders must pass single file; the temples, the tank, the jail, the palace, the birds, the carrion, the Guest House, that came into view as they issued from the gap and saw Mau beneath: they didn't want it, they said in their hundred voices, "No, not yet," and the sky said, "No, not there". (pp. 323–5.)

With that refrain "Not yet" the educator for world understanding could knit together for his pupils this fifth novel with the first. He could quote Ulrich's words: "His view was that in this century we and all humanity are on an expedition, that pride requires that all useless questionings should be met with a 'not yet' and that life should be conducted on interim principles, though in the consciousness of a destination that will be reached by those who come after us" (Vol. I, p. 45).

It is surely to that consciousness of a destination that education for world understanding should contribute, and at the adult level it may most successfully do so through the medium of the novel.

CHAPTER 5

THE TERRESTRIAL TEACHER

> What I want to do, in short, is to express the psychology—the mixed feelings of pride, hope, disappointment, expectation of the man who sees himself no longer as a Frenchman, or a Chinaman but as a terrestrial.
> (TEILHARD DE CHARDIN, *Letters from a Traveller*, p. 133.)

What I want to do in this chapter is to express the psychology of the terrestrial teacher. What kind of a man or woman does he or she need to be? Let us try and answer this question first in quite general terms and then in a variety of particular situations, which by their very nature make pedagogical demands in education for world understanding.

The terrestrial teacher is neither a saviour nor a "stooge": that is to say he is able to resist those pressures in any society, which either tend to force him into a messianic role, a figure that will solve all the problems unsolved or neglected by doctors, priests and parents, or which relegate him to a kind of child minder, dog's body, second class citizen, undervalued and despised. Instead he will choose to be a witness in and outside school to those truths of education for world education, which we have been examining in previous chapters. This means that he needs to be firmly rooted in the particular context in which he is operating but capable of uprooting himself and teaching under different circumstances should the opportunity or the need arise. He must, in the words of Sir Fred Clarke, be "of the type" of his pupils and their parents and at the same time "beyond the type". He must not only be a person with a sense of reality but also one with a sense of possibility. Unless the latter has some roots in the former he is "a Man without Qualities" (see the previous chapter); unless the former has some sense of the latter he too is "a Man without Qualities". He must have escaped from what Charles Davy has described in *Towards a Third Culture* as the "onlooker-consciousness", must be deeply involved in the travail of his times and yet mature enough to transcend it. Thus he can fulfil his other function as a rock against which his pupils may beat and so in the shock of encounter discover who they themselves really are. Yet his very "commitment to more consciousness (and in some degree we are so committed) must come to terms with the inherent limitations of consciousness many people show" (G. H. Bantock, *Education in an Industrial Society*). Finally he must be able to manage a double loyalty, to his own local community with its particular needs and beliefs and to that supra local, supra-national, one world, without the orderly functioning of which, as we have already seen, no local community can any longer survive. Sometimes this effort will lead to his discomfort and even to his professional and personal martyrdom, but for this he must be prepared—it should be part of his training.

It is instructive to lay alongside these suggested criteria the "recommendation concerning the status of teachers item 18.3 of provisional agenda of the fourteenth general conference of UNESCO—Paris—November 1966":

Guiding Principles

   III. Education from the earliest school years should be directed to the all round development of the human personality and to the spiritual moral social cultural and economic progress of the community as well as to the inculcation of deep respect for human rights and fundamental freedoms; within the framework of these values the utmost importance should be attached to the contribution to be made by education to peace and to understanding, tolerance and friendship among all nations and among racial or religious groups.

   IV. It should be recognised that advance in education depends largely on the qualifications and ability of the teaching staff in general and on the human, pedagogical and technical qualities of the individual teachers.

   V. The status of teachers should be commensurate with the needs of education as assessed in the light of educational aims and objectives; it should be recognised that the proper status of teachers and due public regard for the profession of teaching are of major importance for the realisation of these aims and objectives.

VI. Teaching should be regarded as a profession; it is a form of public service which requires of teachers expert knowledge and specialised skills, acquired and maintained through rigorous and continuing studies; it calls also for a sense of personal and corporate responsibility for the education and welfare of the pupils in their charge.

VII. All aspects of the preparation and employment of teachers should be free from any form of discrimination on grounds of race, colour, sex, religion, political opinion, national or social origin, or economic condition.

VIII. Working conditions for teachers should be such as will best promote effective learning and enable teachers to concentrate on their professional tasks.

IX. Teachers' organisations should be recognised as a force which can contribute greatly to educational advance and which therefore should be associated with the determination of educational policy.

The teacher must know so well what he exists to teach and love it so well that he is ready to make certain sacrifices in defence of his vocation. All of this will be futile if he cannot communicate his message, he must be a master of the pedagogical arts and crafts, the kind of teacher so nobly envisaged by Martin Buber in *Between Man and Man*. Speaking of the teacher's relationship to his pupils Buber writes:

"Interference divides the soul in his care into an obedient part and a rebellious part. But a hidden influence proceeding from his integrity has an integrating force", and he adds, "when I fail as a teacher of character, it is because I have made the fatal mistake of giving instruction in ethics." By contrast Buber then gives us the following pen-picture, which may form a useful bridge from our general to our particular reflections. It may be taken as the prototype of the series of pedagogical situations we shall be going on to discuss.

For the first time a young teacher enters the classroom independently. ... The class before him is like a mirror of mankind, so multiform, so full of contradictions, so inaccessible. He feels, "these boys—I have not sought them out; I have been put here and have to accept them as they are—but not as they now are in this moment, no, as they really are, as they can become. But how can I find out what is in them and what can I do to make it take shape?" And the boys do not make it easy for him. They are noisy, they cause trouble, they stare at him with impudent curiosity. He is at once tempted to check this or that troublemaker, to issue orders, to make compulsory the rules of decent behaviour, to say no, to say no to everything rising against him from beneath. And if one starts from beneath one perhaps never arrives above, but everything comes down. But then his eye meets a face which strikes him. It is not a beautiful face, nor particularly intelligent; but it is a real face, or rather, the chaos preceding the cosmos of a real face. On it he reads a question which is something different from the general curiosity: "who are you? and do you know something which concerns me? do you bring me something? what do you bring? . . ."

And he addresses this face. It says nothing very ponderous or important, he puts an ordinary introductory question: "what did you talk about last in geography? The Dead Sea. Well, what about the Dead Sea?" There was obviously something not quite usual in the question, for the answer he gets is not the usual schoolboy answer; the boy begins to tell a story. ". . . and everything looked to me as if it had been created a day before the rest of creation." Quite unmistakably he had only in this moment made up his mind to talk about it. In the meantime his face has changed. It is no longer quite as chaotic as before. And the class has fallen silent. They all listen. The class too is no longer a chaos. Something has happened. The young teacher has started from above.

Before proceeding to consider some specific situations, two points need to be kept in mind: first, that for comparative purposes we shall be applying the same three criteria of judgement to each situation, namely the transcendence of national sovereignty, the problems exemplified by the food and population control situation, and the necessity of emphasising shared human values; secondly, that in such situations terrestrial teachers will feel themselves in an agonising dilemma, namely how much to compromise with the pressures of those in society who contradict their own global loyalty.

Situation 1. *In the Midlands of Britain*

Recently the population of a certain industrial city has had added to it several thousand non-white immigrants. Their children have entered primary school, and they will soon be taking their places in increasing numbers in the secondary schools. They are not a homogeneous company, as they consist of West Indians, Pakistanis and Indians: some of their families have come to stay, and maybe are already second generation settled British citizens; others are in Britain only for a working spell. Linguistically the English of a few is excellent, of most sketchy and often taking (to the English ear) unfamiliar speech rhythms, of a sizeable minority very poor indeed. Their religious affiliations include at least Hinduism, Buddhism, Islam and Christianity: their economic situation with few exceptions is lowly; they bring a wealth of different cultural and social customs into the heart of a long-established English way of life.

Against the background of such facts as these let us picture Form IIIb tackling "the Expansion of Europe from the 16th to the 19th century". Our terrestrial teacher will need to deal with topics such as the slave-trade and the British conquest of India. Seated in front of him are the children of men and women whose fathers were at the receiving end of this imperialistic process side by side with their white peers whose forefathers were the conquistadors and entrepreneurs of Western investment. He is teaching his subject in an age which has witnessed the attainment of national independence in the West Indies, India and Pakistan with all the grandeur and misery which that achievement has brought in its train. If he is a skilful pedagogue he will try and explain both the positive and negative aspects of the 200- or 300-year period of European dominance, pointing out the benefits bestowed as well as the exploitation indulged in, and then deliberately elucidating the ways in which human collectivities do in fact expand the span of their political consciousness and allegiances (see Charlotte Waterlow, *Tribe, State and Community*). Indeed he may well find it opportune and expedient, if the rapport between him and his class is as good as it should be, to bring the whole story to a climax in the here and now of the existing school situation. "Here we all are", he might sum up, "British citizens of the mid-twentieth century owing one particular loyalty to what concerns us in our own country and another one to that global community of which we are fragments, locally joined together, but whose future existence depends on our ability to piece the political bits, white, black and brown, together in order to establish a functioning world political unit."

Our second, ever-present constant of reference, namely the food and population problems of the world, can very easily be approached, though both, being highly emotionally toned subjects, require the teacher's most deft and delicate touch. Why does Ahmed never eat pork and prefer boiled rice to porridge? Young children's ability to tolerate this kind of difference is often not very great—it can easily and quickly degenerate, especially under prejudiced adult pressures, into a contemptuous jeer to the effect that "niggers eat Kit-E-Kat". But what an opportunity for the sympathetic and well-informed teacher to operate with lessons on eating to live as compared with living to eat, on what constitutes a balanced diet, while this has been and in many regions still is unattainable, and how therefore it has come about that different people in different climates have concentrated upon different kind of foodstuffs. A lesson or two on the work of the Food and Agricultural Organisation and the World Health Organisation can appropriately follow, together with an introduction to the work of Oxfam. Only at sixth-form level, or possibly in specially devised courses of domestic science and home economics for school leavers, would it be wise to attempt any systematic treatment of the personal and collective implications of population control.

Once again a local colour variable has been connected and can be seen to be connected to a multi-racial global constant.

"E don't believe nuffink really." This comment by a 13-year-old English schoolboy, whose household though nominally Church of England never dreams of practising the Christian faith, provides an apt introduction to consideration of our third constant of reference, the spiritual one. This boy was echoing, somewhat inelegantly the barely formulated convictions of his fellow countrymen that not to be Christian is tantamount to not being religious at all and that therefore all non-Christians are at best non-believers or at worst dagoes or cultural inferiors. Here again our terrestrial teacher has an opportunity for interpretation. To begin with he can get genuine and responsible upholders of the Christian, Islamic, Hindu and Buddhist faiths to come into the classroom and expound their respective beliefs in simple words. He can show the children the film on "World Religions" obtainable from the Parliamentary Group for World Government. He can help his pupils to distinguish between the somewhat similar ethical demands of the various religions, the Golden Rule, as distinct from their diverse philosophical assumptions, such as pantheism or monotheism. He can above all invite the class to recognise the reality of one value, potentially shared by all humans irrespective of colour, race or creed, namely that which links together and sustains relationships between human beings beyond though related to their physical and intellectual affinities. What quality is it that makes it possible for Jo from Trinidad or Indira from the Punjab to say to Bill from Birmingham, "I believe in you"?

(*Note.* The Council of Christians and Jews has produced a gramophone record, which makes a fine teaching aid for any class trying to come to terms with racial prejudice. One side depicts the search of a non-white student for lodgings and his rejection at the door, the other of a young Jew attempting to become a member of an exclusive golf club near London.)

Situation 2. *In a School of the European Community*

As a Frenchman, German, Italian, Dutchman, Belgian or Luxembourger, the teacher we are now considering may be assumed to have himself been educated and to have started his professional career in France, Germany, Italy, the Netherlands, Belgium or Luxembourg. If, as may further be assumed, this man or woman is in the age bracket 27–34, he or she belongs to the post-Second World War generation, though his or her superior—say in the age range 50–60—belongs equally firmly to the pre-1939 era—a formidable obstacle to their mutual understanding. All their pupils were born after 1945, but many of the parents of these children will themselves have been victims or executioners in the Second World War. The school community of which they, the adults and the children, are the human ingredients, has been constituted as a result of the coming into existence of the European Common Market and the promise of the creation of a European community.

Entering the secondary school classroom one morning in Varese or Mol or Luxembourg Monsieur X or Fraulein Y is faced with the following question, posed shall we say by 15-year-old Angelo

Pini, native of Milan: "How can Germany really belong to our European community when half of her lies outside it to the East?" In his reply our teacher, as a good European and terrestrial, will seek to set the problem of German reunification in its historical, ideological and contemporary contexts. Against the background of the general growth of the nation state he will say something about Germany's retarded nationalism, her rapid industrialisation and urbanisation at the end of the nineteenth century, how she came to be divided as part of an Allied deal during the Second World War and how today her reunification depends on the degree to which Europe and the West as a whole attain unity. In other words, he will seek to answer his questioner by saying in effect, "She can't, because contemporary political realities demand a united world if there is to be a united Europe large enough and therefore capable of containing a united Germany".

Alternatively our teacher could find himself involved in a discussion of the relationships between the EEC and some of the Developing African countries: "What on earth have I got to do with Senegal?", pipes up a girlish voice in the unmistakable dialect of southern Bavaria! Let him answer her in some such words as these:

Originally it was not intended by the creation of the Rome Treaty to include anything to do with overseas territories, but the French insisted that they should. . . . So it was decided that the Treaty should include an association with the overseas territory of a neutral state, and a separate treaty was signed for five years. . . . In 1965 this agreement was renewed after the first five years and this time these eighteen African territories signed the agreement themselves—there was no question of France signing for them because by this time they had all become independent. The main characteristics of this agreement are that they, the African territories, have certain advantages in the European market, they get the benefit from the reduction of tariffs between the European countries towards one another, while it is possible for them to so protect their own infant industries. Also they will get a programme of aid over the five years of 730 million dollars, to help them build roads, bridges, railways, schools and hospitals and other less spectacular but no less useful things like wells within their villages. (p. 252: *Since 1945: Aspects of Contemporary History*, General Editor: James Henderson, Methuen, 1966.)

So once again the terrestrial teacher has here an opportunity of demonstrating that "no man is an island entire unto himself"—

not even a Bavarian schoolgirl! European manufacture and African trade are closely interwoven in the emerging pattern of world economic order.

Thirdly, there can well arise a question to do with the apparent conflict of values, especially religious or ideological ones. Perhaps our teacher comes upon two pupils, Belgian and Dutch, in hot dispute about their basic beliefs. Maybe behind the former there stretches a past history of passionate attachment to the Flemish and Roman Catholic cause, while behind the latter there has accumulated a formidable array of North Holland Calvinism.

"The community is Christian or it is nothing", cries the Belgian. "What you mean", replies the Dutchman tauntingly, "is Roman Catholic or nothing!" And then, at that tense moment, our terrestrial teacher has to intervene decisively.

"You are both wrong and you are both right", he might begin. "In so far as Europe is civilised, it is so very largely by reason of its Christian inspiration, Protestant and Catholic, but that Christian faith is not shared, at any rate in its metaphysical aspect, by more than a minority of Europeans today, and Christianity itself in the world as a whole only constitutes a portion of the beliefs of men. Just as Protestants and Catholics have had to learn to sink their differences in the face of a common enemy (witness their comradeship and solidarity in the concentration camps), so Christian and Non-Christian in Europe and in the larger world outside have to sink their ideological differences if they are to survive as a species. Now, let me ask each of you to declare what the values are, which you think all human beings have in common?" By means of this kind of response our teacher will once again have touched a constant framework of reference for global man, this time the spiritual one.

In a Middle East Refugee Camp

Ever since the emergence of the state of Israel there have been thousands of Arabs, exiled from their former homes, living in the UNWRA camps of Jordan. Here successive generations of young people have been born and received their schooling—the majority as adults to remain there, a fortunate, gifted, determined minority to get out and find employment elsewhere. Let us imagine our terrestrial teacher at work in one such camp school. It is a hut or collection of huts on a site exposed to the extremes of heat and cold, inadequately equipped as regards desks, books and blackboards. Its pupils are drawn from households, which are starkly housed and ruled over by embittered and frustrated elders: food, on a relief basis, is just adequate, clothing drab and adult morale consistently low. Outside the camp, the wider world can only be viewed through the distorting spectacles of the never-ending feud between Arab and Jew, blazing or smouldering.

As occasion arises at different age-levels, whether as part of a History or Social Studies course or in out-of-school activities, the teacher, identifying himself with his pupils' hopes and fears, as he must do to a very great extent if he is to gain their confidence, might attempt some such approach as the following to our three "constants of reference".

"Look! Whether we like it or not, and most of us obviously don't, we must start beginning to understand the contemporary world scene from the situation in which we find ourselves. We are refugees. Where from? What kind of things made us into refugees? The Israelis have a case for their attitude. Let us examine and decide just how sound or unsound it is. Nationalism is rampant throughout the world: just how much of it can the Middle East indulge in without committing collective suicide? Does a solution of seemingly intractable problems as between General Nasser, the Knesset and the rulers of the other Arab states lie in some kind of Middle Eastern Federation? If so, what would be the conditions of its coming into being?" It may well be that even in ventilating such political thoughts the teacher is going too far, not remaining sufficiently of the type to preserve the type's confidence. Perhaps all he can hope to do is to provide his pupils with the opportunity to study comparative nationalism as a global phenomenon and to leave them to draw their own conclusions.

As for the economic constant of reference, our teacher and his pupils have a laboratory specimen on their own doorstep, namely the vast irrigation project for making the desert to blossom, at present fatally compromised by the Arab–Israeli dispute regarding the waters of the Sea of Galilee. What is called for here is a strictly objective analysis of the irrigation needs of Israel and her Arab neighbours from the point of view of food-production.

Ideologically and religiously our teacher will strive to explain the nature and scope of the triple encounter between Judaism, Islam and that kind of materialistic humanism which accompanies the technological penetration of the whole of the Middle-East area whether Arab or Jewish.

Linking together all these three constants of reference, which the teacher is trying to keep steadily before the attention of his refugee pupils, is the significant presence of the United Nations Organisation in the Middle East. This is indeed a rare chance to achieve a pedagogical ideal, namely to start with the growing-point of interest of the child—in this case his political sterilisation, his economic depression and his cultural alienation—and to establish the connection between these particulars and the early strivings of that embryo of world government, the United Nations Organisation. Lesson material of a rich and colourful variety can be assembled from the archives of the UNWRA and of UNSTO as a branch of UN Peacekeeping Machinery. The fact that peace in our times is a bloody business can be tellingly illustrated by drawing on the pages of Von Horn's *Soldiering for Peace*. From a discussion of the problems he had to face in the H.Q. in Jerusalem there can emerge the general problem of creating some kind of World Police Force and the extent to which it needs to have teeth, i.e. to be armed. In brief the terrestrial teacher trying to follow his vocation in the context of a Middle East refugee camp is terribly handicapped and gloriously aided: non-educational influences in the shape of racial hatred and enmity must emasculate much of his striving, but the United Nations Organisation "presence" can give a point and punch to his education for world understanding, which his colleagues elsewhere may envy.

In Apartheid South Africa

Whether he is of British, Afrikaans, Bantu, Indian or "Coloured" extraction, our terrestrial teacher can only operate, if he is to remain active and out of gaol, within very strict limits. His pedagogical spirit must find itself "cabined, cribbed, confined" because the entire South African context is aimed at racial segregation and the maintenance of White domination, both of which are incompatible with any kind of peaceful world order. Nevertheless, within the interstices of a near totalitarian regime there are opportunities for education for world understanding: some of them are well worth noting and honouring. (See *UNESCO Report on the Effects of Apartheid on Education, Science and Culture in South Africa*, 1967.)

On the White side two publications should be mentioned as courageous attempts to keep burning the flame of independent thought. One is *Prejudice in the Classroom* by Eleanour Howarden (Johannesburg, 1966), in which we read:

> ... if African peoples are presented to school children solely as engaged in unprovoked attacks on white farmers—and this is the picture which most South African textbooks and teachers present in both primary and secondary schools—then though the facts of individual attack may be correct, the total impact on the students and the picture they form of past events, is untrue. It omits the attacks by Europeans, the provocation suffered by the Africans, the loss of their lands, the courage and chivalry with which the Ame-Xhosa fought in defending their country from invasion.

Another publication is F. E. Auerbach's *The Power of Prejudice in South African History* (Cape Town/Amsterdam, 1965) which reveals that in the Transvaal no junior book explains land tenure and its relationship to frontier clashes as one of the key aspects of early South African history.

Further evidence of resistance educationally to the implications of apartheid is still to be found in the English-speaking universities, the Press and the Churches: one university lecturer, himself under house arrest after a spell in prison, is now permitted just to go to and fro between his apartment and his lecture-room to teach but is not permitted to enter his own Senior Common Room: nevertheless his voice is not silenced. Most remarkable of all perhaps is the admirable work of the Johannesburg, Cape Town, East London and Port Elizabeth branches of the World Education Fellowship By encouraging an interest in education outside South Africa, by inviting speakers from Europe and the U.S.A. to tour South African educational institutions and by occasionally effecting some slight pedagogical liaison with non-White teachers, this organisation sustains the morale of its members. Men and women like those associated with activities such as these are true terrestrial teachers, even if they are prevented from open and explicit advocacy of those parts of education for world understanding, which would immediately result in their arrest.

Turning now to the lot of the non-White teacher, it is essential to be reminded of the exact and horrific handicaps under which he pursues his profession. In 1965 the salaries paid to African teachers were less than half those earned by white teachers— 41·9 per cent for men and 37·9 per cent for women. In 1965 the gap widened when White teachers' salaries were raised. The material amenities of most of the non-white schools are manifestly inferior when compared with those of the Whites.

> Africans are required to finance their own educational institutions to a very large extent through special taxation on them, which limits the range of subjects offered to them in school and which isolates South African children of different ethnic groups from each other ... overcrowding and an insufficient number of teachers—for the most part poorly trained —add to a pattern which serves to prevent Africans and to lesser extent Coloureds or people of Asian extraction from playing a full role in society. (Apartheid, *The Unesco Courier*, March 1967.)

And yet in spite of all this there are non-White teachers in South Africa, worthy in every respect of the epithet "Terrestrial", in that they offer steadfastly, admittedly narrow, means whereby some of their pupils can begin to peer out beyond the confines of township and reservation, can be brought into contact, however cursorily, with a few of the great human documents of the liberty of the mind, can be given technical skills which will some day rebound to their own people's advantage and link them in confidence to the rest of the technologicalised planet.

One such man is the headmaster of the secondary school in an African township, a man of strength and compassion, already well beyond bitterness, who uses the often absurdly irrelevant academic curriculum of his school to direct the attention of his pupils to the sources of knowledge which can help to make them free. Bringing a visitor into the classroom of one of his senior forms, he remarked quietly: "More girls than boys at the moment, because the boys are still sleeping off their drunkenness outside in the school yard: several girls who won't be here next term; they'll be mothers by then. Let me introduce my friend and colleague who is teaching them Latin grammar! You smile at the incongruity and irrelevance of the subject under these circumstances! There is no need to: for some it is the gateway to materialisation of all that may lie beyond for them in the shape of release from poverty, oppression and crime. Surely this is better than nothing?" And from the expressions in these children's faces as they gazed at their headmaster, the visitor knew that this must be true.

Another such man in an Indian school in Natal is the English master. He explained to a visitor that his class of 17-year-old boys and girls had just finished reading Shakespeare's *Antony and Cleopatra*: they were about to discuss its characters. One girl ventured the opinion that no woman, not even Cleopatra, was worth man's dishonour or his country's disgrace. Much argument ensued, by the end of which, thanks to a few deft touches from the teacher, the discussion had broadened to take in the whole question of women's rights in society past and present, references to Joan of Arc, Florence Nightingale, Eleanor Roosevelt and Madame Curie —whole vistas of emancipation in thought and custom opening up, at the end of which this teacher certainly saw visions of a free and united humanity. He too did not, because political circumstances prohibit it, teach about the brotherhood of man irrespective of race and class and creed, but with the help of Shakespeare and those Indian adolescents' own most proper concern with their own loves and hates, he did succeed in stimulating their personal growth, which must inevitably bring some of them into the arena of political awareness and obligation.

A third example, this time a woman, is that of a lecturer in a teacher-training college for "Coloureds": her students in training were going to devote themselves to young children in primary schools at the very onset of their preparation for a long life of being discriminated against by the laws of the land. "We can", she told her visitor, "really only hope to achieve two things with these future teachers. We can ensure that they possess the necessary pedagogical expertise to train their pupils in elementary skills, which may ensure their ability to scrape a livelihood, and secondly we can offer them while they are with us in college the ingredients of a lasting gaiety of spirit." Seeing her visitor's puzzled expression, she added: "I mean by this that we can introduce them to certain sources of nourishment in music and painting and literature, which will redeem the drabness and dangers of their life as teaching members of a coloured community, itself looked down upon by Whites and Indian, envied by the Bantu, and everlastingly tortured by its own undetermined, inferior status. I play them Bach, I show them Picasso, I read them Bernard Shaw. They must get to know a few of the ways to world culture." Under the inspiration of such a terrestrial teacher as this lady, they undoubtedly will.

In a Moscow Classroom

Deep in the heart of communism there are two convictions, which lie very close indeed to education for world understanding. One is the notion of justice for the underdog, and the other is the belief in the power of economic circumstances decisively to influence cultural achievement. Yet any Communist country must by definition be more or less of a police-state with little or no place for the ideological deviant. Our would-be terrestrial teacher in it is therefore confronted with the following dilemma: either he prescribes for an education leading to world co-operation on Marxist terms or he keeps silent on the subject except for gestures he is permitted to make to certain admitted masterpieces of culture in the hope that they will speak out clearly for themselves. Nevertheless, and even when imprisoned within this predicament, he can and sometimes does break the bonds of such theoretical restraint and thereby become, if only implicitly, a terrestrial teacher.

Three instances may illustrate this point. As portrayed in the dialectic of history the individual person, however famous, is seen to perform a different function than when viewed in non-Marxist terms, whether secular or religious. Yet Cromwell, Napoleon and Lenin are presented to Ilytch and Natasha as mighty figures and their qualities of drive and dedication commented on with approbation. Each is thought of as a key catalyst in the revolutionary ferment at work at any one time in England, France or Russia. The Soviet teacher possesses his ideological framework of reference for the interpretation of the ways in which society evolves and definitely comprehends it as a global phenomenon. Non-Communists will disagree with the emphasis he expresses, particularly the kind of built-in determinism of events, but unless they are hopelessly parochial they cannot deny the validity of some of the Marxist insights: to that degree these two kinds of teachers are terrestrial together.

A second instance from a Moscow classroom has to do with the exploration of space. Every Soviet child is imbued from the earliest moment with a passionate concern for scientific growth and development and rightly made to feel proud of his countrymen's pioneer work as cosmonauts. In so far as the Soviet achievement in this sphere is related to what other countries, especially U.S.A., are doing on similar lines, these teachers, who are informing their young of the ways and means by which such technical triumphs are brought about, are helping to create that vast new interstellar perspective in which the unity of our tiny planet becomes blatantly manifest. In their advocacy of the dedication to scientific truth in the laboratory there need be no conflict of loyalties in their pedagogical activities.

The third instance is best illustrated by the following anecdote. Standing in a Moscow classroom was a visiting British teacher:

while the children were writing an exercise he and their young language mistress engaged in a long discussion of certain educational problems. After a while the discussion became animated, then positively heated as both parties brought their ideological guns to bear on such issues as nuclear weapons, the reunification of Germany and—fiercest of all—the deliberate indoctrination of the young, virtuously repudiated by the Englishman, capably acclaimed by the Russian. In a moment of exasperation the former indulged in this ill-conceived and somewhat melodramatic remark: "If these children in the classroom here had been the kids in Budapest who threw bottles at the Soviet tanks when they were suppressing the Hungarian rising, you wouldn't have fired on them—that would have been to outrage every instinct, pedagogical and human, that you so obviously possess." After a short pause, the young Soviet teacher leant on her desk, and quietly retorted: "And the children of Hiroshima . . .?" At that moment the spirits of these two teachers met; each knew as absolutely as anyone can ever know anything that their treatment of children would never be anything but compassionate, loving and non-violent. They had forged, almost by accident, a terrestrial bond which held against ideological difference.

This suggests the further reflection, namely that most misunderstanding between Communists and non-Communists is due to a failure to perceive the difference between the true and the perverted values of Marxist and anti-Marxist doctrine. No serious and responsible Soviet citizen would seek to justify the morality and politics of a totalitarian ant-heap: no serious and responsible American citizen would seek to defend the licence of unbridled liberty. Applied to education, this becomes even more apparent: the order requisite to the promotion of academic study is no different in a Moscow classroom than in one in San Francisco, however different the means by which it is obtained and sustained. The way in which learning occurs is globally valid however varied may be its local manner of functioning.

In East–West Dilemma

Let us consider finally an extreme situation, the respective predicaments of a would-be terrestrial teacher at work in Johnson's U.S.A. and Mao's China. As has already become apparent, that kind of predicament arises harshly enough in South Africa, the U.S.S.R. and the Middle East and more mildly in Europe and Great Britain, but for the reasons we shall be looking at, it is the prospects facing our American and Chinese colleagues which appear to be most acutely antithetic to each other.

In the U.S.A. there are certain general traditional influences at work in society, associated with what is deemed to be—"a good American"—a complex amalgam of strict New England Puritanism, go-getting business success—"little mid-Westernism"—consciousness of Great Power responsibility, immense wealth, pockets of poverty, Democracy with a capital D and Presidential rule, a conviction, now slightly shaken, that there is no problem in the world that cannot, sooner or later, be "fixed" by human ingenuity. Within this framework operates the teacher in some kind of "neighbourhood" school, itself largely under the control of dominant local parental opinion, which supports the general American way of life as painted in the few phrases above, but just because it is parental opinion always tending to be politically Right rather than Left of centre.

The first problem confronting our terrestrial teacher consists in the fact that every interpretation of world events that he may put forward, which is implicitly or explicitly critical of U.S. governmental policy is apt to attach to him the label of Communist, an epithet synonymous with bad, dirty and dangerous.

Originally aimed against the U.S.S.R. this directive has begun to shift more against Red China, while accommodation is now the objective of U.S.–Soviet relations.

The second problem follows from the first, namely how to teach the laws regarding national sovereignty, food and population and the human values as set out at the beginning of this book without running into the crippling frustration of either evading these important topics by keeping silent about them or being written off and possibly dismissed as a "Commy" if the implementation of these laws is commended. Let us take three instances, noting carefully just how far it may be politic for the teacher to go without falling into either trap.

To the south of the United States lies the small independent nation, called Cuba, ruled over by Castro. Only a few years ago it nearly precipitated a head-on collision between the two great world powers of Russia and America. In a high school discussion-class on contemporary "isms", one of the teenagers asked an explosive question: "If Castroism is just the same as Communism, and our boys are fighting Communism in Vietnam, why aren't we fighting the Cubans?" The teacher has a number of careful and delicate issues to deal with here, and he must proceed in the knowledge that some of the homes of his pupils will be reckoning it a pity that the Americans are not at war against Cuba, while others will be advocating the withdrawal of U.S. troops from Vietnam: the majority in a muddle anywhere between these two extremes. Perhaps the most he can do without rousing such resistances as would annihilate his work as a teacher is first to establish the fact with a number of illustrations from other parts of the world that ideological Communism and national Liberation movements are not synonymous; secondly, to offer a quick, vivid character-sketch of Castro and Ho Chi Minh themselves as individual personalities; thirdly, to indicate that in the world of the second half of the twentieth century when and where Great Power interests really clash, both are bound to retreat in the face of threatened escalation from local war into global genocide.

A second instance could be taken on constructive lines from the total corn-producing capacity of the United States: how much is produced annually, at what a cost to whom; how much of it is exported, where to and at what price or free? Answers to such questions should lead on to the general question of the world's food resources as a whole, the present use which is made of them, the problem of their economic and morally justifiable distribution and the relative role of the U.S.A. in the whole operation as compared with other countries—the manifest need for a World Joint Food Production Board to make sense of the ongoing activities of the WHO and the FAO.

A third instance in the psychological field offer perhaps greater opportunities and hazards than the previous two; contrasting types, the "swell guy" and the "good comrade" are brought under consideration, Colonel Glenn and Gagarin for example. By setting these American and Russian figures into a wider context, adding perhaps personalities from Asia and Africa, the teacher can hope to establish some distance between these men and their oversubjective, evaluating students. Secondly, he can raise the whole question of the nature of human motivation, what makes a man or woman take risks, national, ideological, religious? Is it lust for adventure or some ideal of discovering something new and so possibly benefiting his neighbour? Thirdly, he might get his class to sort out what values the "swell guy" and the "good comrade" or even the "decent chap" possess in common and also where they diverge. Have they sufficient in common to be able to trust each other? What is the essence of trust?

Such, it may be suggested, is the quality of education that our terrestrial teacher in the U.S.A. might aim to achieve without offence to the community of which he is a member—charitable interrogation rather than dogmatic statement.

In turning our gaze now on to the predicament of the would be "terrestrial teacher" in Red China, we must be fully aware that his faith, if it is to be expressed at all, can only find outlet, unless it is to be promptly smothered, (a) through the medium of the country's re-creation in Marxist terms and (b) through the cultivation of individual relationships. The formidable immensity of this assignment is well illustrated in a book by Tung Chi-peng and Humphrey Evans, entitled *The Thought Revolution* (Leslie Frewin, 1967). In an article headed "Growing-up in Mao's China" in the *Observer* of 5 March 1967, extracts from that publication indicate two contrasting ways forward for the good Chinaman, who is both patriotic and terrestrial in his loyalties. One is the way chosen by Tung Chi-peng himself, who defected to the West; the other is that of his friend, Hu, who because of or in spite of the fact that he is the son of a real industrialist's son, chose to stay and make his career under the Communist regime. This friendship is the revealing symptom: it reveals each of them as men of good will, but our terrestrial teacher, if he is to retain a respect for and hearing from his pupils, will have to identify himself with the latter. Let us listen to the last words of Hu to Tung Chi-peng before they parted:

> Hu was pleased that he had been made a Youth League member. Considering his background, this was an achievement. He was more successful than I with the Hu technique.
>
> "I'll guarantee that within three years—four at the most—I'll be a Party member," he said.
>
> Then, while I was still speechless with surprise, he said, "But what about you, old Tung, are you going to defect?" I nodded.
>
> "When you get out, make a career of telling the Westerners the facts about Communist China," he said. "Make them understand that we don't have Communism here, or even Socialism. We live under a feudalistic military dictatorship as primitive as this country has had in three millennia."
>
> We walked along in silence. Then he said: "You understand that even if I had the chance to defect I would not take it. Unlike you I *can* survive here. In fact, within 15 or 20 years I'll be one of the leaders."
>
> "But isn't your class background against you?" I asked.
>
> He chuckled. "Even now you are confused by what the leaders say they are and what they actually are. Despite my supposedly unacceptable background and despite the fact that my immediate superiors know fairly well what my sentiments are, they will do nothing against me."
>
> "Our leaders have established a simple, old-fashioned warlord autocracy using witch-doctor mumbo-jumbo. To compete with the modern industrial nations, huge numbers of technicians are needed. Anyone trained to the necessary degree of technology, however, can see through their mumbo-jumbo. So the people needed most by the regime are the most disaffected.
>
> "In my case, there are a growing number of politicians who take my ideas as their own. I don't care. I have ideas and they don't. My security is based on the number of people whose status comes from taking credit for what I create."
>
> "Isn't it dangerous?"
>
> Hu shrugged. "To me it seems less dangerous than taking my chance in a foreign country," he said. "But I want you to tell those outside that we exist. Every day our number increases, and every blunder the 'leftists' make establishes our position more strongly. Look what is happening in Russia. I'm convinced that the same will happen here even faster."
>
> "You make me want to stay and join your group," I said.
>
> "Please don't," Hu said. "When I'm on the Central Committee I'll invite you back for a big celebration. Meanwhile get as far away from here as you can."

THE TERRESTRIAL TEACHER 105

From this passage a clue can be derived as to the possibility of education for world understanding in Communist China: it lies along the same route as that taken already by the U.S.S.R., namely the absolute claim of technological expertise as the passport to an understanding eventually with the non-Communist world. In other words, the basic human constants, now almost entirely obscured by the ideological variables, have a chance of re-emerging via the technological constants. It is surely the task of the terrestrial teacher, labouring in such circumstances as those, to ensure that they do.

The facing of teachers' realities in this chapter compels us to close these reflections on a sober note. Two obstinate facts darken counsel still: one is the fact that in large parts of the world the teacher is not at liberty to speak freely about the truths of the international situation; the other is that it is still only a minority, and in many countries a tiny minority, of children growing up, who possess the mental and emotional equipment requisite for even an elementary understanding of world issues.

This must not be allowed to result in apathy or despair. Readers of the foregoing should have been enabled to make up their minds as to how many of the variables in human habits and experience will have to be sacrificed if an adequacy of global constants is to be obtained. That really is what the whole book is about.

As Franz Kafka once remarked: "Perhaps there is only one cardinal sin, impatience. Because of impatience we were driven out of Paradise; because of impatience we cannot return."

The terrestrial teacher must also beware of this sin and not permit his impatience to become an infection but rather act as a spur to the patient and enduring education for world understanding of all his young.

CHAPTER 6

THE PROMISE OF COLLECTIVE MEMORIES

AN ATTEMPT will now be made to penetrate more deeply into human motivation, to the very sources of that energy which drives the various educational activities we have been discussing. This means trying to understand how human beings form images of the reality of their existence and how those images in turn affect the modes of that existence. Above all it should prove useful to investigate some of the stimulus situations which often release unpremeditated, instinctive behaviour—ways of acting which, however capable of being rationalised, do in fact proceed from traditionally engraved predispositions. More particularly, these can then be related in educational terms to the types of human behaviour that govern the conduct of world affairs.

Because they are the earliest experiences we have of anything, many of our behaviour patterns derive from the experiences we and our forefathers have had of relationship to the parent figures. These are determined by a complex combination of personal, cultural and archetypal factors, all three of which, as we consciously or unconsciously remember them, as we picture their images, influence our attitudes to those set in authority over us long after childhood. The more aware we can become of such influences the more we can control them and discipline ourselves to submit to those that are legitimate and to resist those that are not—the test of legitimacy in the context of our present study being whether or not they conduce to world understanding. This greater awareness can be gained from recognising how the archetypal factor is constant, the personal factor almost limitlessly variable and the cultural factor a semi-permanent but not unchanging mixture of both constants and variables.

Let us take examples of each of these in turn before passing on to consider some exercises in recognition, which should form part of our educational programme.

With regard to the personal factor in relationship to a mother or father this is so variable that all we need note here is first that the attachment of a child to his parents is hardly ever equally strong, he tends to cleave with special devotion to either one or the other; secondly, that there is always an ambivalence of love and hate between them; thirdly, that the intensity of these feelings can differ very greatly, and fourthly that in the degree to which this personal parental relationship is not realised, it tends to be projected on to alternative parent figures, whether public or private, by way of compensation.

With regard to the archetypal factor, what has to be borne in mind is that behind the images of each individual mother and father figure there loom the older, more instinctive, primordial, collective images of motherhood and fatherhood. Moreover, these are frequently fused, though in concealed form, with the personal and cultural images. Each has its positive and negative aspect, the "White Madonna" and the "Black Madonna", the gracious life giving goddess and the devouring witch; the just, wise lawgiver or breadwinner and the oppressive tyrant or bully. Mythology is full of such larger than life figures: they are the common parents of mankind, readily activated when the other two ingredients have for any reason proved inadequate.

With regard to the cultural factor this has to do very largely with the kind of values attached by any particular society to the role of women, also to the structuring of family and household and the kind of employment in which the father of the family is engaged. However, as in most societies, there has always been a strong emphasis placed on filial dependence and obedience, the constants are stronger than the variables. In our own times there has been occurring a sometimes shocking encounter between traditional family patterns as observable in the developing countries and those in the so-called developed ones, the most sensational feature of which has been the challenge by the young of both sexes to the traditional maternalisms and paternalisms—with, however, it must be honestly added, a tendency for these to have substituted for them the paternalism of State or Party. So far as education for world understanding requires acceptance of certain shared cultural values, one of these must clearly be the value set by the world's young on its parents.

It would seem sensible therefore to give all children an introduction to the way in which we form images of our parents, the three components of them and the manner in which any situation, which is a stimulus one for us because of its association with one or both of our parental images, can release instinctive, uncontrolled and possibly destructive behaviour. Here then are a few instances which may be included in such an introduction.

One of the most celebrated women in history is the Hapsburg Empress, Maria Theresa. The interest of her public function and personal character is such that she is inevitably included in any survey of European development and thus forms part of what most potential teachers have learnt something about and will themselves have to teach to others. The following passage could well serve as a starting-off point for consideration of the manifest content of her career as an object of historical and psychological study:

> Maria Theresa saw her duty in terms of history. She was the mother of her people and the guardian of the past. Although she had fostered reforms, she was opposed to change. In this lay one of the chief causes of misunderstanding with her son. Joseph was a revolutionary governor. He adored change, and, unlike his mother, he had a vivid conception of the future. Their difference was not only in wills, but in essential ideas. Yet ideas in a monarch do not stir the love of his people, and with all Joseph's advanced notions about government, he never won the loyalty which was given to his mother. With all her stubborn will, her conservatism and her prudishness, Maria Theresa was a Hapsburg monarch, untroubled by theories. This the people understood. Perhaps the most enchanting scene in which she is revealed in relationship with her people is one that occurred at the time of the birth of Leopold's first son. The ancestral voices spoke to her with gratitude, and when news reached the palace in the evening, Maria Theresa ran out into the street, careless of how she looked, towards the Burgtheater. She went into the royal box and, without pausing to think of the players, announced in a breathless

voice: "Der Leopold hat ein Bube! Der Leopold hat ein Bube!" Her motherliness, the broad Viennese dialect in which she spoke, and her apparent excitement smoothed away the memory of taxes and wars. Joseph's theories and innovations were dull compared with her matriarchal graces. (Constance Lily Morris, *Maria Theresa: The Last Conservative*, pp. 300-1, London, 1938.)

Here is an example of the problem of the relationship between individual and movements in human history and their respective influence on one another, as shown by such a phrase as "the mother of her people and the guardian of the past". It is not hard to perceive that she was by no means all good or all bad, either in her personal life (relationship to Joseph) or in her diplomatic encounters (the Polish Partition): as a mother and ruler she had her negative and positive aspects—her "matriarchal graces" evidently possessed certain psychological resonances.

Growing familiarity with the facts of Maria Theresa's personality and her historical role may cause one thing and most surely will cause another. It may happen that one or other of the pupils will relate the mother-figure of the Empress to his own or to an acquaintance's mother or to one in fiction. If this occurs, the skilful teacher can make capital delicately, even draw an object lesson to do with maternal possessiveness or deprivation. What must happen is that the unconscious, both individual and collective, of all the pupils will be at work on the manifest content and contribute to the "creative fantasy activity" of their minds. It is here that the teacher has a big role to play: it is for him progressively to amplify the material from the particular case of Maria Theresa to other particular cases and then to the general, collective figure of the Great Mother. By his aid the students will encounter her first in mythology and legend, so becoming aware there of her various manifestations (Ishtar—Cybele—Isis) or the range of possible archetypal mother motifs operating in their own psyches. Above all they will be helped to come to terms with, having first learned to recognise, the inevitable ambivalence with which all children must regard their mothers. The "good" mother acceptable to consciousness—the Madonna, Alma Mater, nurturing, fostering and sweetly possessing, must be contrasted with her obverse side—

the "bad" mother, unacceptable and therefore banished by the individual and most societies for a long time to the unconscious—the Witch, the enchantress, "Madame La Guillotine"—terrible and annihilating.

A piece of history often taught in schools and presumably familiar to any educated European is the Revolt of the Netherlands against Spain in the second half of the sixteenth century. The students may be invited to refresh their memories of that event, so that they possess the necessary background for the following well-known passage from Motley to have meaning for them:

William the Silent

He went through life bearing the load of a people's sorrows upon his shoulders with a smiling face. Their name was the last word upon his lips, save the simple affirmative with which the soldier who had been battling for the right all his lifetime commended his soul in dying "to his great captain, Christ". The people were grateful and affectionate, for they trusted the character of their "Father William", and not all the clouds which calumny could collect ever dimmed to their eyes the radiance of that lofty mind to which they were accustomed, in their darkest calamities, to look for light. As long as he lived, he was the guiding-star of a whole brave nation, and when he died the little children cried in the streets.
(J. Motley, *The Rise of the Dutch Republic*, Vol. III, Part VI, Chapter VII, p. 481, London, 1889.)

What evidence, it may then be asked, is there of bias in this interpretation? What kind of picture are we being asked to accept of "Father William"? Does the cheery benevolence of it square with other facts we may know about the character of William the Silent? What would a Spanish or Roman Catholic version of the story be like? To what extent can we hope to know him as he really was? What qualities of fatherhood generally did Motley take for granted in his attempt to identify ruler and nation?

By means of these and other questions and their discussion at the level of the manifest content of the material a climate will have been produced in which the latent significance of it can begin to operate. Only very occasionally—and then not to be artificially encouraged—will any one of the pupils bring through the latent into the manifest by making some such remark as, "Oh! but I think fathers are always bound to be feared". The real work is accomplished by the teacher so handling the manifest content as to provide the means whereby the unconscious attitudes of the pupils to their own fathers can contribute together with the archetypal primordial father-images to stimulate that "creative fantasy activity" which is the objective of the whole exercise.

That objective can be considered to have been attained when the student has, as a result of achieving a synthesis from his or her conscious and unconscious responses to a particular father, been enabled to understand the role of the father-figure generally and to appreciate the myriad different forms which it assumes, why some will need to fear and some to love this figure when they encounter it in their elders. This means among other things that the students will appreciate the function of the patriarchal figure in mythology and legend as it gradually began to stand more and more for the principle of consciousness. They can thus come to realise the profound meaning of the Oedipus story, i.e. that the actual or symbolic killing of the father is an expression of the death-wish against customary law and coercion—it is the inspiration of the rebel spirit. They can be brought to see in the father-figure the archetype of law and order, the conservative preserver whose perpetual role it must be to challenge his children by his power and whose penalty it is to be overcome by them. God, Pope, king, judge, and even headmaster—these the trained teacher with his new accession of consciousness can relate to healthily, confident in being able to discriminate between the personal and the archetypal father-figure for himself and so indirectly aiding his pupils to do the same for themselves when the time comes.

In turning next to images of the hero and his enemies we need to remind ourselves of just how potent the imprints of images on our consciousness are and how, once made, they so largely condition our reactions when we find ourselves in similar or analogous situations to those in which they were first created. An obvious example is the similarity of imprint, widely separated in time, of Henry V's heroic exhortation to his fellows and Field-Marshal Montgomery's heroic exhortation to his followers, the one in 1415, the other in 1945. Another example is the British newspaper, the

Daily Mirror and its comic strip, where the hero figure appears in the shape of Garth. Such images are caused, strengthened, modified—perhaps even obliterated for a while—by the physical and psychological associations connected with them. This becomes plain when we understand that "the stages of the hero myth have become constituent elements in the personal development of every individual" (Joseph Campbell, *The Hero with a Thousand Faces*, p. 131). In other words, each individual on his journey through life re-enacts, however modestly, the triple pattern of the hero's evolution, separation—initiation and return. There is or can be a correspondence between the heroic career objectively observed and personality growth subjectively experienced. That is why an appreciation of the constants and variables in the hero–enemy image and then the deliberate opting for the composite hero–enemy image appropriate to the needs of contemporary world society must form an essential part of education for world understanding. In his book, *The Ulysses Theme: A Study in the Adaptability of a Traditional Hero*, W. B. Stanford provides fascinating, detailed evidence of this phenomenon:

> Turn by turn this man of many turns, as Homer calls him in the first line of the Odyssey, will appear as a sixth-century opportunist, a fifth century sophist or demagogue, a fourth-century Stoic: in the middle ages he will become a bold baron or a learned clerk or a pre-Columbian explorer, in the seventeenth century a prince or a politician, in the eighteenth a Philosophe or a Primal Man, in the nineteenth a Byronic wanderer or a disillusioned aesthete, in the twentieth a proto-Fascist or a humble citizen of a modern Megalopolis. (p. 4.)

The pedagogical conclusion to be drawn from this premise is that at various stages of their schooling children should be introduced to a variety of heroic types, always paired with their necessary adversaries. Each category would then be illustrated by characters taken from the mythology and history of a wide range of global cultures.

> His (the hero's) characteristic theme is the quest, the adventure, the great deed. It is he who fights the dragon, is swallowed by and destroys the sea monster, encounters and worsts the false knight, rescues the maiden, frees the captive, delivers the waste land, discovers the priceless treasure. He is magically armed and equipped. Arthur has his sword,

By courtesy of the National Gallery.

In this painting of St. George and the Dragon, Ucello has portrayed the chief primordial images of man—the archetypes.

Girl	*Dragon*	*St. George*
Anima	Animal	Animus
Lover	Instinct	Lover
Goddess	Shadow	Hero
Madonna	Devil	Warrior

In the background: the dark cave of Origin——the Bright Heaven of Illumination

Excalibur, Roland his Durandel, Perseus has the Gorgon's head, Siegfried his cloak of invisibility; there is the bow of Ulysses and the bow of Robin Hood; and a whole stable of magical and demonic horses, from Pegasus to Rosinante, Sleipner to Black Bess. Jason and the Argonauts seeking the Golden Fleece, Hercules and his labours, Orpheus, Ulysses, Aeneas descending to the land of the shades, the Archangel Michael in his conflict with the power of darkness, St. George slaying the dragon, the Knights of the Round Table in the quest of the Holy Grail, all are so many facets of the hero and the heroic task. (P. W. Martin, *Experiment in Depth*, pp. 104, 105.)

From the grand variety of candidates for treatment it would be wise to select those heroes for inclusion in the syllabus, who represented different types, and different epochs of the world's history and different geographical regions. Each would necessarily be presented together with the opposition that confronted him, and this of course would precipitate that crisis of judgement and paradox that is always occurring when one man's enemy appears as another man's friend, e.g. that "Devil Wilkes", who was also the "champion of liberty". That, however, is the tragic element in human destiny, which it is essential to absorb into the curriculum if education is to be realistic and if, in every age and specially the age of one world or none, man is to learn to judge correctly which of his contemporary tragic choices are legitimate and which are not. "In truth, slayer and slain are one, but, upon the stage on which creation is played out, they are enemies, and the slayer has committed a sin; it is such a sin as the heroes of Greek drama committed—one that could not be avoided, and yet in which atonement is required" (Gai Eaton, *The Richest Vein*, p. 58).

In this kind of context the following suggestions may indicate the scope of selection for the teacher:

Heroes of National Liberation:	Bolivar and the Spanish
	Kenyatta and the British
	Sun Yat Sen, Chiang Kai-chek, Mao Tse-tung and their enemies
Heroes of Exploration and Discovery:	Christopher Columbus and his Enemies (human and national)
	General Fawcett and the Jungle

Heroes of Art and Science:	Leonardo da Vinci
	Marx
	Freud
Heroes of War:	Hannibal
	Genghis Khan
	Attila
Heroes of Peace:	Lord Boyd-Orr
	Count Bernadotte
	Hammarskjöld

From an understanding of the conflict in which such characters have been involved, teacher and pupils should gradually acquire the capacity to apply suitable criteria of the heroic to the contemporary world problem: the hero is he, who in spite of nationalist passions, struggles to initiate the transcendence of political national sovereignty; the hero is he, who in the face of human poverty and apathy, promotes the growth of more food and limitation of population: the hero is he, who solves the problem of "rendering the modern world spiritually significant" (Campbell, *op. cit.*, p. 388). In these ways we can procure a vivid image of the hero of our times and by contrast know how to recognise, fight and love his enemies, who are the fanatical nationalist, the economic exploiter and the "hollow man".

When we come next to the images of friend and lover, we touch the most intimate and often the most powerful of all stimuli situations because these characters lie close to the sexual, emotional desires of men and women. The "collective memories of mankind" are full of Helen and Cleopatra, Antony and Paris: every culture pattern has an easily identifiable model of the feminine and masculine ideals; each individual has his or her "pin-up" of the girl friend and the boy friend. Into public life private emotional relationships keep on intruding, whether for better or worse, Parnell and Kitty O'Shea, Catherine the Great and her succession of lovers. Group loyalty is closely linked to sexual and emotional loyalties: trust between friends and lovers is an essential condition of trust between peoples. What pedagogical use can therefore be

THE PROMISE OF COLLECTIVE MEMORIES 115

made of the personal, cultural and archetypal factors in the human relationship of love and friendship?

Two actual historical characters and two psychological mechanisms may be mentioned by way of illustration. The first of these is that of Lawrence of Arabia:

> The world naturally looks with some awe upon a man who appears unconcernedly indifferent to home, money, comfort, rank, or even power and fame. The world feels not without a certain apprehension, that here is someone outside its jurisdiction, someone before whom its allurements may be spread in vain; someone strangely enfranchised, untamed, untrammelled by convention, moving independently of the ordinary currents of human action, a being readily capable of violent revolt or supreme sacrifice, a man, solitary, austere, to whom existence is no more than a duty, yet a duty to be faithfully discharged. He was indeed, a dweller upon the mountain tops where the air is cold, crisp, rarified, and where the view on clear days commands all the kingdoms of the world and the glory of them.
> Lawrence was one of those beings whose pace of life was faster and more intense than what is normal. Just as an aeroplane only flies by its own speed and pressure against the air, so he flew best and easiest in the hurricane. He was not in complete harmony with the normal. (The Home Letters of T. E. Lawrence and his Brothers. From *The Allocution*, by Winston Spencer Churchill, Blackwell, 1954.)

Most members of the group will have heard something of this extraordinary character, and tutor and students should be able to move easily into a brief review of Middle Eastern affairs with particular reference to that period of awakening Arab nationalism with which Lawrence himself was connected, and so providing a colourful lesson. The material should yield, at the level of manifest content, much useful debate about the qualities of leadership in general and what it was in particular that made the First World War Lawrence's hour, and what it was in the aftermath that prevented him from continuing his public career. As discussion closes in on the possible causation of his individual tragedy, the latent significance of his figure may even begin to emerge; it will certainly find a certain resonance in the individual and collective unconscious image of the masculine principle. Lawrence's personality is an almost classic example of most of the main ingredients which constitute the Animus, woman's largely unconscious primordial image of the masculine—monk, priest, crusader, wise man, undifferentiated he-man, dedicated scholar—all these and other manifestations of the masculine principle of questing consciousness may thus be aroused through association. Moreover, Lawrence's personal fate witnesses to what happens to an unrelated consciousness—it cannot sustain the normal; either it becomes inflated by identifying itself with that which is far greater than itself (Nietzsche and the Superman) or it seeks safety in flight (as Lawrence in the R.A.F. and on his motor-cycle very literally did for a time).

He may be compared and contrasted with other animus images, e.g. the character of Mr. Greatheart in Bunyan's *Pilgrim's Progress*. From a pedagogical point of view the object of the exercise is to familiarise the students of both sexes but particularly the girls with the idea that every male figure has two components, one being the person he genuinely is and the other a hook on which may be hung the projection of the largely unconscious male fantasy figure of woman. Mr. Jones, the art master, and "darling" or "dreadful" Daddy are not only themselves but also vessels of the Animus archetype.

The second example is that of Mary Queen of Scots:

> So the mystery of Mary Stewart remains a mystery to this day. That she was cognisant of the plot to murder Darnley is the more probable theory, in view of facts which no one denies; yet those facts remain intelligible if she was innocent. There are no admitted facts which preclude her guilt: none which prove it conclusively. The various confessions of interested witnesses, voluntary or extorted, are untrustworthy. The genuineness of the Casket Letters is doubtful. No opportunity was given for cross-examining the witnesses or examining the letters. The world believed that Mary was guilty, however it may have been disposed to condone the guilt. The world was probably right. But to pretend that there was a fair or complete investigation—that Mary's guilt was proved before the Commission—is absurd. That Mary from first to last protested against being brought to the bar of an English tribunal—whose authority she could not acknowledge without implying a recognition of that suzerainty which Edward I of England had claimed, and Robert I of Scotland had wiped out at Bannockburn—was entirely compatible with the innocence of a high-spirited and courageous princess: and would have been so, even if she could have counted on the absolute impartiality of her judges. Knowing that she could count on nothing of the kind, fully aware that Elizabeth herself would in fact be the judge, and suspecting with very good reason that any verdict pronounced by her would be

shaped strictly with a view to her own political convenience, it is almost inconceivable that Mary should have acknowledged the jurisdiction merely because Innocence in the abstract ought to invite enquiry. Had Mary been less beautiful, less unfortunate, less of a heroine of romance, it is likely enough that she would find few champions; but the pretence that she had a fair trial would still be none the less untenable. (A. D. Innes, *England under the Tudors*, p. 279, Sixth Edition, London 1920. Cf. Schiller's *Maria Stuart*, now delightfully accessible in the English translation by Stephen Spender.)

This short, quite prosaic passage, which could of course be replaced by almost any number of alternatives, would suffice as manifest content for this part of the exercise. That the Queen in her lifetime made passionate enemies and lovers and that, ever since, she has had eager advocates and stern critics, these are themselves facts which should aid the process by means of which the pupils can familiarise themselves with examples of the mechanism of projection in both history and personality. By the method of discussion and amplification of an archetypal theme they may once again be brought to appreciate the distinction between individual lever and primordial feminine image.

Furthermore, such considerations can lead on to a proper evaluation of the relationships between the sexes in the context of twentieth-century society. The schoolmistress, trained in elucidation of the archetypes, Animus-Anima, should be able to realise that she herself is in a hot Animus temper when she exclaims, "I can tell you I gave 4C a piece of my mind". The schoolmaster should be able to recognise an Anima mood when he remarks, "Can't think what possessed me to be so soppy with the VIth". Both can then take corrective measures with benefit to themselves and their pupils.

Enough has been said to make the point that an understanding of the motives and mechanisms of behaviour as between friend and lover and illustrated by copious examples from the great love stories of fact and fiction, should form another essential part of education for world understanding. The just balance between the masculine and feminine ingredients of human personality is a vital condition for a healthy social organism or the reasons already noted in the Introduction, this requires to be a global one, a shared sexual ethic, an universal respect for the "Other" and possibly the gradual growth of miscegenation as a positive good rather than a doubtful product of expediency.

The second oldest and deepest "collective memory of mankind", only to be exceeded by that ultimate one governing what he thinks his life is for, is the archetypal image of evil, the dark thing or shadow which threatens his identity. It manifests itself in each of the three previous categories of image, the parental, the heroic and the loving, and its supreme manifestation is of course the phenomenon we know as death. Each culture-pattern has its own model of what it deems evil; each individual has his *bête noire*; the shadow is the necessary concomitant of the light. Because, however, it is always threatening and in the end always destroys both our bodies and our egos we dread it. We seek to deal with it by projecting it on to others, trying to escape from it and denying its reality, but in vain except in so far as we have grown a shadowless part of ourselves, namely spirit, classically defined in the following lines of the *Gita*:

> Never the spirit was born, the spirit shall cease to be never:
> Never was time when it was not, end and beginning are dreams:
> Birthless and changeless and deathless, the spirit endureth for ever,
> Death doth not touch it all, dead though the house of it seems.

For most human beings, however, their bodies and their ego-identities have been the be-all and the end-all of their existence. By means of the projection mechanism they attribute to others the defects of their own bodies and egos and discover scapegoats in others for their own shortcomings or crimes. This explains the connection between human images of evil—the enemy over there —and the way in which these can stimulate negative, primitive attitudes towards others. The classic case in our own times is, of course, Hitler's treatment of the Jews as an expression of the complexes of frustration in German society of the 1920's.

The role of evil, the shadow and the "inferior function" in human affairs must therefore claim a place in our curriculum of education for world understanding. An example from Old Testament history may help to make the meaning of this section clearer.

The story of Jacob and Esau provides a particularly clear and striking parable of the shadow. What impression does the old Hebrew tale make? The indivisibility of man and his shadow is plainly announced:

> Two nations are in thy womb and two manner of people shall be separated from thy bowels.
>
> Esau was a cunning hunter, a man of the field; and Jacob was a plain man, dwelling in huts.
>
> The face is Jacob's face, but the hands are the hands of Esau.

Jacob and Esau represent two different but complementary types of individual and also two complementary though opposed facets of a single personality: each is necessary to the other. (See Appendix for a detailed lesson scheme based on this approach.)

A second example is chosen deliberately from very recent history with the idea of posing to all student-teachers the greatest problem of society in the modern world, namely that of totalitarianism. Just because such men and women are too young to remember the Second World War as part of their own conscious memory, it is all the more important that they should obtain some insight into this most tremendous of all social conflicts by means of an appraisal of the Hitler phenomenon. The following passage provides an admirable piece of manifest content:

> In this age of unenlightened despotism Hitler has had more than a few rivals, yet he remains, so far, the most remarkable of those who have used modern techniques to apply the classic formulas of tyranny.
>
> Before the war it was common to hear Hitler described as the pawn of the sinister interests who held real power in Germany, of the Junkers or the Army, of heavy industry or high finance. This view does not survive examination of the evidence. Hitler acknowledged no masters, and by 1938 at least he exercised arbitrary rule over Germany to a degree rarely, if ever, equalled in a modern industrialised state.
>
> At the same time, from the re-militarisation of the Rhineland to the invasion of Russia, he won a series of successes in diplomacy and war which established an hegemony over the continent of Europe comparable with that of Napoleon at the height of his fame. While these could not have been won without a people and an Army willing to serve him, it was Hitler who provided the indispensable leadership, the flair for grasping opportunities, the boldness in using them. In retrospect his mistakes appear obvious, and it is easy to be complacent about the inevitability of

his defeat: but it took the combined efforts of the three most powerful nations in the world to break his hold on Europe.

Luck and the disunity of his opponents will account for much of Hitler's success—as it will of Napoleon's—but not for all. He began with few advantages, a man without a name and without support other than that which he acquired for himself, not even a citizen of the country he aspired to rule. To achieve what he did Hitler needed—and possessed—talents out of the ordinary which in sum amounted to political genius, however evil its fruits. . . . Hitler was indeed a European, no less than a German phenomenon. The conditions and the state of mind which he exploited, the malaise of which he was the symptom, were not confined to one country, although they were more strongly marked in Germany than anywhere else. Hitler's idiom was German, but the thoughts and emotions to which he gave expression have a more universal currency. (Alan Bullock, *Hitler. A Study In Tyranny*, Epilogue, p. 735.)

Subsequent discussion with the pupils would seek to elucidate from within a German setting three aspects of a contemporary tendency to social disease, which is more indeed than a purely German phenomenon. These are first the very nature of totalitarianism, secondly the impossibility of it being resisted by traditional methods of statecraft and thirdly the need for a creative response to its challenge. This essentially democratic response must be such as to be capable of accepting the daemonic elements inherent in it and so by transcending them to pass beyond resistance.

Faustian man has need of Mephistopheles in his quest for self-knowledge: the shadow which his being casts takes on the form of an objective reality, apparently external to himself. The integration of his personality occurs where that is assimilated which was previously projected, thus in the language of Blake, "destroying the negative to redeem the contraries". It may well be that Europe and many other parts of the world stand in need of the German example as the means whereby they can learn how to redeem their own bodies politic by accepting the daemonic forces within them.

The introduction of the idea of transcendence is deliberate and is intended in the sense conveyed by the following extracts from Gabriel Marcel's *Men Against Humanity*.

But let us imagine then, the situation of our own country immediately after a Putsch or *coup d'état*: if rebellion is futile and a retreat into insignificance impracticable, what, supposing that we are fully aware of our situation, does there remain for us to do? At the risk of discontenting and even of shocking those who still tend to think of solutions for political problems in terms of positive action, I shall say that in that region all the ways of escape seem to me to be barred. Our only recourse can be to the Transcendent: but what does that mean? "The Transcendent, Transcendence", these are words which among philosophers and intellectuals, for a good many years past, have been strangely misused. When I myself speak here of a recourse to the Transcendent, I mean, as concretely as possible, that our only chance in the sort of horrible situation I have imagined is to appeal, I should perhaps not say to a power, but rather to the level of being, an order of the spirit, which is also the level and order of grace, of mercy, of charity; and to proclaim, while there is still time, that is to say before the state's psychological manipulations have produced in us the alienation from our true selves that we fear, that we repudiate in advance the deeds and the acts that may be obtained from us by any sort of constraint whatsoever. We solemnly affirm, by this appeal to the Transcendent, that the reality of ourselves lies beyond any such acts and any such words. . . . What we have to do is to proclaim that we do not belong entirely to the world of objects to which men are seeking to assimilate us, in which they are straining to imprison us. To put it very concretely indeed, we have to proclaim that this life of ours, which it has now become technically possible to make into a hideous and grimacing parody of all our dreams, may in reality be only the more insignificant aspect of a grand process unfolding itself far beyond the boundaries of the visible world. In other words this amounts to saying that all philosophies of immanence have had their day, that in our own day they have revealed their basic unreality or what is infinitely more serious, their complicity with these modern idolatries which it is our duty to denounce without pity: the idolatry of race, the idolatry of class, . . . a man cannot be free or remain free, except in the degree to which he remains linked with that which transcends him, whatever the particular form of the link may be, for it is pretty obvious that the form of link need not reduce itself to official and canonical prayers. (pp. 15 et seq. (Harvill Press, 1953).)

What then, the pupils may be asked, is the nature of this psychological wisdom, which was so largely lacking for example in the German resistance movement to Hitler and which does not as yet seem particularly evident in democracy's resistance to the Communist form of totalitarianism? It lies, as the perennial philosophy has consistently taught, in the recognition that man is a whole, that psychic wholeness is the natural condition of the individual and the collectivity, towards which state they both of them are pointed but from which they are for ever deflected by the forces of their own ignorance. In recent years the science of psychology, it could be pointed out, has begun to make available some information as to the way in which this ignorance is bred, chiefly by the light it has thrown on the reality and power of the unconscious. Analytical psychology in particular has shown how modern man needs to become aware of the personal and collective unconscious below the surface of his mind, on which he is largely dependent, and without the acceptance of which he is nothing but its slave. Nowhere is this more apparent than with reference to that part of himself which his consciousness regards as inferior or bad in so far as it is aware of it at all, and which is generally projected unintentionally on to some other enemy or foreign devil. Where no such object is legitimately available, as for example the mediæval devil, the shadow has to fall elsewhere—on nation, class or creed—and when once this process is at work the forces of reason and conscious prudence are helpless. This has been the dominant force in Germany and in most of western civilisation increasingly since 1914, and it is this force which underlies the manifold economic and political upheavals of the twentieth century. By an understanding of it we can obtain a clue as to the basic nature of totalitarianism.

Here, the pupils should be reminded, it is necessary to distinguish clearly between totalitarianism and the various kinds of authoritarian dictatorships which have existed from time to time in history. The former is a modern phenomenon and is essentially of European origin. It is the expression first of the individually and collectively unsolved problem of the shadow, secondly of the rise to power of the pseudo-educated masses, and thirdly the rapid industrialisation and urbanisation of previously rural communities. It expresses the reaction of large social groups away from the perhaps as yet excessive challenge of democratic responsibility and back to dependence on authority figures, which themselves are then endowed with the attributes of parental and shadow archetypes which control the movements of the group from the depths of its unconscious. As Ernst Toller once put it: "The desire for a dictator is the desire for castration."

In inviting the pupils to consider next how the totalitarian situation may be avoided or resisted, an apparently political problem will serve to illuminate an educational one, namely that of totalitarianism in the school with its symptoms of violence and delinquency. By its nature totalitarianism only establishes itself when the political, economic and psycho-spiritual condition of society is of such a kind as either by the sins of commission or more often those of omission to invite it. This means that once established with all the equipment of modern power at its disposal, a totalitarian government cannot be resisted effectively from within by any of the traditional methods of conspiracy and that, if it is overthrown from without by alien conquest, its essential ingredients—those which originally brought it into being—are not destroyed but only and very temporarily driven underground. Resistance is beside the mark unless the instruments of that resistance themselves partake of the mystique in a complete sense of which totalitarianism is its daemonic shadow part. Dr. Zimmer in a lecture entitled *Integrating the Evil* has expressed this truth quite clearly:

> The power of evil cannot be crushed or defeated by counter aggression. It has to be checkmated by the mere sight of a superiority attained by self-conquest and self-sacrifice: by the mere sight of a plenitude acquired through the integration, in a recognisable form, of its own black essence. The power of evil has to be made to collapse and dissolve in despair of its own vain, purely destructive nothingness: otherwise after it has regained its strength and has stripped away the fetters of its under-world dungeon, there will be another war. Every lack of integration in the human sphere asks for its antagonistic co-operation. (Lecture No. 39, Guild of Pastoral Psychology, London.)

Finally we would do well to meditate on what is involved in the transcending of totalitarianism both in the individual boy and girl and in society collectively. If totalitarianism has its roots in the undue psychological frustration of individual and collective instinctive drives, in the economic contradictions of capitalist society and in the political inadequacy of the conventionally liberal forms of representative government, then, where resistance is impossible, only transcendence remains.

This to the modern ear somewhat off-putting word, transcendence, brings us to the last image of which we need to take stock. The "collective memories of mankind" are full of what it has believed concerns it ultimately—Paul Tillich's definition of religion. This traffic with the numinous also has its imagery like the other archetypes considered in this chapter: it has a distinctively religious tone. *The Masks of God* (see J. Campbell's three volumes under that title) are many, but, however diverse their appearance, they cover a basic similarity, namely "the metaphysic that recognises a divine Reality substantial to the world of things and lives and minds; the psychology that finds in the soul something similar to, or even identical with, divine Reality; the ethic that places man's final end in the knowledge of the immanent and transcendent Ground of all being . . ." (Aldous Huxley, *The Perennial Philosophy*, p. 1).

This means that, according to our formula, education for world understanding must provide opportunities for children to learn about the archetypal, cultural and personal factors which have gone to the creation of these pictures. They need to gain insight into the beliefs of the traditional creeds together with the most up-to-date interpretations of them, into the substitute creeds such as belief in the State as God and into the variety of alternative panaceas such as Science, Existentialism, Pacifism, Spiritualism, New Messiaism or Racism. Here above all future world citizens require to recognise and reverence the constants in human belief and to be prepared to so modify the variables as to remove from them their elements of militant fanaticism. This probably implies a readiness to accept shared values rather than to insist on uniformity of belief. As John Dewey remarked in 1929: "The problem of restoring integration and co-operation between man's beliefs about the world in which he lives and his beliefs about the values and purposes that should direct his conduct is the deepest problem of modern life." In a recent book Barbara Ward has been making this same point:

> We cannot tell what will follow from so new a voyage of discovery. But it at least contains the possibility that all round the world the views of life which have tried, in Paul Tillich's phrase, to give man a "dimension of depth" may be found to possess in common (and hence strengthen and enhance) some profound insights into human predicaments and hopes.

THE PROMISE OF COLLECTIVE MEMORIES

... Most religions see a living link between the depths of man's being and the ground of all existence—however expressed. And all, even the secular Confucians, have believed, ever since the great moral revolution in the millennia before Christ, that the ultimate law of man's being is a moral law, reflecting a larger harmony in the whole universe—a harmony the Chinese described as "the way of heaven" and Dante as "the love that moves the sun and the other stars".

If these are the common insights into man's "dimension of depth", then clearly every one of them directly contradicts the basis instinct of nationalism—every one of them depends for its validity on the fact of a humanity, a dignity, and a value common to all mankind. It is therefore possible that the new journey of discovery made by religious men may uncover a new opposition to frantic tribalism and give a sense of rootedness to the vision of human dignity and human freedom that no utopian ideology could hope to provide. The other aspect of the revolution may not be new but to-day it seems to be gathering momentum. It is an attempt not simply to map and define "the dimension of depth" but to discover it and live in it. Beyond the barriers of class and creed and race and nation there live our fellowmen—not dummies, not abstractions, not enemies but living breathing men who are neighbours, men in want, in confusion, men in anger and rejection, men to whom their fellows must reach out, men with whom they must discover not in theory but in practice what it is to share the human substance. Young people off to the Peace Corps, worker priests in the slums of Paris, young Komsomols volunteering for schools in the Arctic, nuns in Calcutta giving starving beggars off the streets the privilege of a decent death—the examples are world wide. They make up pockets of a new élite who are so far beyond our angry nationalisms, that like the just men of the Talmudic legend, their profound humanity may well hold up the rooftrees of heaven for all mankind. (Barbara Ward, *Nationalism and Ideology*, pp. 123–4 (Hamish Hamilton, 1967).)

We have been arguing that the identification and deliberate study of those images, which form the stuff of the "collective memories of mankind"—the parents, the hero, the enemy, the lover and the ultimate—can contribute positively to education for world understanding. It can do so by revealing how such images once formed act potently on all human beings, shaping their behaviour and tending to produce stereotype reactions to experiences, which appear similar but which are in fact novel and which require to be met with novel methods.

In bringing this book to a conclusion, our final aim must be to try and indicate how a universal education, anchored in that depth of understanding just described, can be applied to the analysis and mastery of world events. Selecting a phenomenon, a place and an institution, each of which has posed problems of world order in the twentieth century, it is hoped to make a fresh contribution to the educational task in hand by demonstrating how such topics can be creatively presented.

1. THE REFUGEE PHENOMENON

> We are like doctors, who hasten to help the injured without seeking to know who caused the injury..." (U.N. High Commissioner for Refugees.)

Refugees are a symptom of the malfunctioning of twentieth-century societies; the symptom itself has in turn given rise to further malfunctioning. This fact received general recognition through the holding of a World Refugee Year, 1959–60, by the end of which and in spite of considerable governmental and voluntary endeavour the problem remained still largely unsolved. The word, refugee, is used to describe those millions of men, women and children, who through war, revolution, or natural disaster have been uprooted from their homelands and sent hurrying across the surface or lodging in holes and corners of this planet, earth. Before attempting a teaching interpretation of this phenomenon let us remind ourselves of its origins and scope. There are four clearly recognisable phases: (1) refugees created by the First World War, 1914–18; (2) refugees from totalitarian oppression, mostly Nazi, during the 1930's; (3) refugees created by the Second World War, 1939–45; (4) post-1945 refugees, the bulk of which were at first European but have become predominantly Asian and African.

Assistance to refugees was first organised under international auspices in 1921 with the appointment of Dr. Fridtjof Nansen (Norway) as League of Nations High Commissioner for Refugees. Not all groups of refugees, however, have been the subject of international action and, for several decades, international or intergovernmental agencies of an expressly temporary character were created to solve each refugee problem as it arose.

The first major international agency which was concerned with refugees and displaced persons after the beginning of the Second World War (1939/45) was the United Nations Relief and Rehabilitation Administration (UNRRA). UNRRA was established on 9 November 1943; its broad objectives included the relief, maintenance, rehabilitation and, ultimately, repatriation of United Nations nationals who had been displaced as a result of the war. However, a large number of these displaced persons were reluctant or unwilling to be repatriated, either because they had lost all ties with their countries of origin, or because of changed political conditions there. These people, together with non-settled pre-war and wartime refugee groups, represented the core of the post-World War II refugee problem in Europe. At the beginning of 1946, it was estimated that there were some 1,675,000 persons who, to all intents and purposes, had to be considered as refugees for whom new homes had to be found.

In the wake of UNRRA came the International Refugee Organisation (IRO). The United Nations General Assembly approved the IRO's Constitution on 15 December 1946. A Preparatory Commission for IRO was established and, on 1 July 1947, took over the functions and activities previously exercised by UNRRA on behalf of refugees and displaced persons. IRO succeeded the Preparatory Commission on 20 August 1948. By the time the IRO had ceased its operations in February 1952, the Organisation had resettled more than a million displaced persons and refugees in new homes throughout the world, had assisted approximately 73,000 to return to their former homelands and, altogether, had given some form of help to more than 1,600,000 persons. Nevertheless, in spite of all the IRO's efforts, and in spite of various provisions it had made for a number of clearly defined residual refugee groups, there remained thousands of refugees (many of them handicapped) who still required protection as well as material assistance when IRO operations ceased.

On 3 December 1949 the General Assembly of the United Nations, recognising the continuing responsibility of the United Nations for the international protection of refugees after the termination of IRO, decided to appoint a U.N. High Commissioner for Refugees.

On 14 December 1950 the General Assembly adopted the Statute of the Office of the United Nations High Commissioner for Refugees (UNHCR). The Office came into existence on 1 January 1951, originally for a period of three years. Since then its mandate has been renewed by the General Assembly for three five-year periods (most recently, until 31 December 1968).

The U.N. High Commissioner for Refugees is elected by the General Assembly on the nomination of the Secretary-General and is responsible to the Assembly: he is at present Prince Sadruddin Aga Khan. (Quoted from a background paper of the UNHCR's office.)

The figures below, supplied by UNHCR, give an arresting picture of the world situation of refugees:

OVERALL REFUGEE STATISTICS 14 February 1966

1. Some 40 to 50 million people have become refugees at one time or another since the end of World War II, but most have been

settled meanwhile, and at present some 10 to 15 million have still not found an adequate basis for life.

2. Refugee groups of concern to UNHCR are the following:

Group	Approximate numbers	Present location
European	7000	Africa and Asia (exc. Far East)
,,	650,000	Europe
,,	1200	Far East
,,	100,000	Latin America
,,	260,000	North America
,,	50,000	Oceania
(rounded) Total	1,070,000	
Cuban	15,000	Spain
,,	25,000	Latin America
,,	235,000	U.S.A.
Total	275,000	
Chinese	1,100,000 (Good Offices)	Hong Kong
,,	80,000	Macau
Total	1,180,000	
Rwandese	50,000	Burundi
,,	25,000	Congo (Kivu)
,,	15,000	Tanzania
,,	67,000	Uganda
Total	157,000	
Angolan	200,000	Congo
Mozambique	11,000	Tanzania
,,	5000	Zambia
Total	16,000	
Portuguese Guinea	50,000	Senegal

Group	Approximate numbers		Present location
Tibetan		44,000	India
"		7000	Nepal
	Total	51,000	
Sudanese		44,000	Uganda
"		18,000	Central African Republic
"		10,000	Congo (Oriental)
	Total	72,000	
Congolese		54,000	Burundi, Central African Republic, Tanzania, Uganda

In addition, UNHCR cared for and repatriated over 200,000 Algerian refugees from Morocco and Tunisia during and after the 1954/62 fighting in Algeria. Also UNHCR resettled 5000 refugees from Togo and facilitated the repatriation of 1500 Kurdish refugees from Turkey to Iraq.

3. *UNRWA*

Palestine Arab refugees	1,250,000*	Middle East

4. *Others*

German (originally 12,500,000)	3,000,000	West Germany
Indian (ex-Pakistan originally 8,000,000)	3,500,000	India
Pakistan (ex-India originally 8,000,000)	3,500,000	Pakistan
Vietnam	1,000,000	South Vietnam
Cambodia	10,000	Cambodia
Congolese	500,000	internal

* The recent Arab–Israeli war has increased the need of refugees in this area, particularly on the East and West of Jordan. In June 1967 it was estimated that there were 400,000 on the West bank and 300,000 on the East bank, making an addition of at least 100,000 to those already there.

Two further extracts from the UNHCR office give a concise summary of major developments in recent years.

Africa

UNHCR has provided assistance to nearly 500,000 refugees in Central, East and West Africa upon the request of the governments concerned and, generally, at the earliest possible stage of a newly arising refugee situation. This aid may range in scope from relatively modest financial contributions needed to help a government to meet the cost of providing food and shelter to newly arrived refugees, to the setting up of a large-scale operation. (Such an operation might include the provision of food, medical services and relief supplies by the League of Red Cross Societies upon the UNHCR's request; supplies from the World Food Programme; other logistical support needed to safeguard life and health, etc.)

UNHCR is, in essence, non-operational and acts as the planner and diplomatic go-between to enlist the help of all those governments, organisations and individuals likely to be in a position to assist in any given refugee situation. UNHCR is thus concerned with the elaboration of plans and projects aimed at making refugees self-supporting as speedily as possible, and programmes, financed with a basic contribution from UNHCR, generally serve as a starting-off point leading to substantial supporting contributions from governments and other sources (see also below).

In Africa, where large areas of virgin land still exist, governments are frequently requested by UNHCR to provide land where the refugees can settle and, invariably, respond most generously. The actual settlement of refugees calls not only for a vast effort by themselves, but also for close partnership between host governments, UNHCR, and those organisations which have the technical knowledge and strength to carry out projects whereby refugees, through their own work and efforts, will ultimately become fully self-supporting members of a new community in regions which, subsequently, may well receive development aid to benefit the population as a whole.

Altogether, over a quarter-million refugees have entered the Democratic Republic of the Congo, including Angolans (some 200,000 new largely resettled), Rwandese (25,000) and Sudanese (10,000). About 50,000 Rwandese refugees are in Burundi. Uganda granted asylum to over 1,000,000 refugees (including some 67,000 Rwandese and some 44,000 Sudanese). In line with the generous policy of asylum pursued by so many countries in Africa, the United Republic of Tanzania accepted nearly 30,000 refugees, mostly from Rwanda (15,000) and Mozambique (11,000).

A noteworthy example of the solidarity shown by African States in assisting each other in seeking solutions to refugee problems was the acceptance during 1965 for permanent settlement in the United Republic of Tanzania of 3000 Rwandese refugees, whose integration in the countries which had first granted them asylum presented certain difficulties.

Their movement was achieved thanks to UNHCR-organised operation which included an airlift, as well as travel by boat, rail and, finally, road to a new settlement area in the Mwesi Highlands.

Other refugee groups in Africa include 50,000 in Senegal (coming from Portuguese Guinea); about 5000 in Zambia (coming from Mozambique).

In addition, about 54,000 persons were displaced as a result of civil strife and upheavals in the Democratic Republic of the Congo, and entered Burundi, the Central African Republic, Uganda, and the United Republic of Tanzania.

Asia

In Macau (where UNHCR opened a branch office during 1965), various types of projects are being implemented for the 80,000 Chinese refugees there. The main effort in Macau is directed at seeking gainful employment for them. As to the 1,100,000 Chinese in Hong Kong, UNHCR has channelled funds in support of the substantial efforts undertaken over the years by the Hong Kong authorities. This has been done on the basis of special General Assembly resolutions.

There are 7000 Tibetan refugees in Nepal (UNHCR opened a branch office at Kathmandu during 1965) and 44,000 in India. The UNHCR programme in Nepal (carried out by the Nepalese Red Cross) is primarily directed towards the refugees' resettlement on the land. UNHCR assistance in favour of the Tibetan refugees in India takes the form of supporting a number of land-resettlement projects undertaken on their behalf by the Indian Government and a number of international organisations.

One further extract from the *Observer* Foreign News Service No. 23850, 16 May 1967, may remind us that in Europe, too, there is an organising problem.

Escaping Season Begins in Eastern Europe

George Black   Rome, May 16, 1967

The small village of Padriciano is not the most beautiful spot in Italy. Western tourists bound for Yugoslavia's beaches and pleasure grounds do not give it a second glance as they pass by. But to travellers coming from the other direction it seems the sweetest place on earth.

At Padriciano there is a centre for fugitives from the "Popular Republics" of Eastern Europe, and to it every year come some 5,000 men, women and children. Most of them do not have a penny in their pockets; and some have no pockets at all, having swum a river, or crossed a lake on an improvised raft to reach Italian territory, and what they hope is freedom, in their underpants.

The number of these refugees from Communist countries has increased every year since 1956, and 18 months ago the Italian Government was obliged to build a big new centre near Trieste to house them until officials reach a decision on their future.

This "waiting room" for the West is five miles from the Yugoslav frontier, a modern, well-designed complex of three-storey buildings which might be a big hospital were it not for the high, spiked concrete wall which surrounds it. Now, in spring, the centre houses little more than 600 people, for the escaping season has barely begun; but all through the summer the numbers will increase. The camp commandant, Signor Stelio Crassnig, expects that last year's record figure of 5,917 refugees will be surpassed.

They arrived, usually in the evening, from police stations in every part of Italy, tired, dusty and emotional. "Viva Italia, viva liberty!" they cry, and tend to throw their arms around the camp gate-keeper who, being a refugee himself, gives as good as he gets. The Italian Carabinieri pat the newcomers on the shoulder, smile and shepherd them away, to one of the camp's three sectors—for families, for single men, and for single women. More than 70 per cent are young men, under 30.

And here the difficulties begin. Food, clothes and sympathy are no problem. The centre is administered through the Ministry of the Interior, and helped by religious organisations, of which the US-backed Catholic Relief Services is the most important.

It has headquarters in Trieste, but if a fugitive seeks political asylum he must have political reasons; many escapers make it plain that they have come "just for the money", and have no particular aversion to and fear no danger from Communism. They are sent back, after a joint international commission, which consists of two Italian and two United Nations officials, has considered their request and found it wanting.

The lucky majority, once asylum is granted, move from the "isolation" blocks to the "free" sector. Now they may leave camp at 9.30 a.m. and return at 10.30 p.m. Not many do, since their only source of income is the 15,000 lire they can earn a month as interpreters, barbers, teachers, gatemen, gardeners, in camp. For a few the temptations of liberty are too much, and there are one or two cases of theft and prostitution yearly in Trieste.

Young girls who have escaped alone are cared for in the camp's "Villa Morning Star", where "Caritas", a Catholic organisation, teaches them English, cooking and other subjects.

The wait may be long; up to a month before the Commission says "yes" or "no"; then three weeks in the "free" sector under surveillance before the refugee moves on to camps at Latina and Capua, for another indefinite wait until departure to the country of their choice can be arranged. The United States, Canada, Australia and Sweden are the top choices—either because of their reputation as lands of promise, or because the fugutives have relatives there. Very few stay in Italy.

The wait can be bitter; not everyone expected to be introduced to "freedom" by way of three or four months in detention camps. But at Padriciano the atmosphere is cheerful, even gay, although there is often fear for relatives left behind.

Dark-haired Gabor Acs, a 19-year-old Budapest student with a handsome face, told me that he had left his parents and two sisters behind. "I dreamed about getting away for years. If you're young in my country you either let yourself be regimented, or you run for it. I told my Dad 'I'm taking a holiday in Yugoslavia this year'. I think he knew I was going when I shook his hand to say goodbye. First I went to Sesana, but someone told me it would be better further north at Kranjska. I got there in the dark and didn't think twice. I just ran across the fields towards the frontier—straight into the Yugoslav police. I was three weeks in jail, then they let me go. 'Too bad for you if we catch you near the border again' they said, and I thought 'That's that'. But in the hotel I met an Austrian commercial traveller who had a big empty trunk in his truck used for coffee—and he took me over in that. We left at nine, and at 9.50 we were in Italy. Now I'm going to Sweden to study law."

I spoke to Karolina Szabo, a lively blonde with bright eyes who did secretarial work. "I tried to get into university, but they refused. My father's a tailor, and he insists on running his own private shop—that counted against our family. And they knew he'd helped in the rebellion of 1956. But Daddy didn't want to leave Budapest. Poor Dad, he hasn't replied to my letters, but it probably doesn't mean anything. I escaped when I went on holiday to Capodistria and met a young German married couple. I told them what I planned, and they said 'there's space in the boot if you want to come into Italy with us', and that's what I did. I was awfully frightened, but I'm glad now. I've got an uncle in Canada and he's expecting me."

Not everyone escapes in such dramatic ways. Since a 1964 tourist agreement between Yugoslavia and the other four major iron curtain republics, many "escapers" have been able to leave their homelands on regular passports, and the number coming from Hungary, Czechoslovakia, Poland and Rumania has risen sharply.

Yugoslavia leads the way still, because it is closest to Italy, and because the number of refugees is swelled by Italians who unwillingly became "slavs" when Marshal Tito obtained a sizeable piece of disputed territory at the end of the war.

Here then is the raw material for our lesson preparation: to complete it, there should be added some instances of actual educational endeavour within the general refugee programme, e.g. in Africa.

PRIMARY SCHOOLING

As a public service, primary schooling is indispensable for groups, such as refugees, where half the population are children. After some months during which classes are held in the open, without blackboards, desks or benches, and with no textbooks or exercise books, the refugees themselves often take the initiative and improvise "bush schools". The teachers, also refugees, often draw no salary.

In some villages, however, financial aid from UNHCR and welfare bodies has made it possible to build permanent schools. This has been done at Kayongozi, Muramba and Kigamba in Burundi, where Oxfam contributed $15,000 for this purpose. At Mwesi in Tanzania the Lutheran World Federation and the Finnish Association for Aid to Refugees have made funds available to build three classrooms, and at Rutamba, also in Tanzania, gifts from Sweden are being used to construct nine classrooms, of which three are already completed.

These schools have the added advantage of being designed to conform with the educational system of the country concerned, so that the government can take over their management and ensure that the curriculum follows that prescribed under the national system. The government provides the services of a headmaster and teachers, and furnishes basic equipment on condition that the refugee settlements agree to pay the direct taxes which, in any case, are very light.

These schools are of course not restricted to refugee children but accept pupils from the surrounding local villages. In this way links which are likely to prove lasting are forged between the indigenous population and the newcomers. Another advantage is that teaching is carried out in the language of the host country, which is not the case in the "bush schools" where the refugee teachers continue to use that of their home country.

Recognising the importance of all these factors in promoting the permanent integration of refugees from different lands, the Executive Committee of the High Commissioner's Programme decided at its session in the spring of 1966, to include provision for primary education in the regular programme of establishing settlement areas. From now on the building of schools will be considered as one of the basic needs.

While new refugee settlements will therefore have schooling facilities from the start, and while as a rule Government schools are being set up in those settlements established before 1966, there are some areas where unfortunately only rudimentary teaching is available to refugees, under conditions which are far from satisfactory.

HCR recently made a survey of the situation which revealed that an outlay of more than a million dollars is required to make good the existing deficiencies. These inadequacies are most glaring in regions where many refugees are concentrated, or where there are no state schools at all; for example, among the refugees from Rwanda and the Sudan in Uganda; at Mugera, where there are 25,000 refugees from Rwanda; or in Senegal, where only 30 per cent of children of school age receive any education. In Casamance province, indeed, the proportion is even less, simply because refugees are concentrated there.

On the other hand, care has to be taken not to give the refugees an undue advantage in the matter of schooling. Educational facilities made available to them must be related to the prevailing national standard.

To be sure when refugees have enjoyed a higher educational level in their country of origin than can be expected in their country of asylum, this gives rise to a problem. A case in point are refugees from Rwanda, who are used to universal primary schooling; and it can be argued under these circumstances that they should be allowed to continue to provide it at their own expense in "bush schools" as long as the formal system cannot do so. In any event, the growth of state schooling is being actively fostered everywhere in Africa.

SECONDARY, TECHNICAL AND UNIVERSITY EDUCATION

While provision for primary schooling is henceforth to be made in refugee settlements, there is a serious lack of facilities for secondary, technical and university education. Although in most of Africa primary education is free for children admitted to the state schools, secondary education is usually only available in far-away towns and is quite beyond the means of refugees. The same holds true for technical and higher education. Local people face the same problem, but they at least have access to scholarships from various sources. (Extract from UNHCR Report *Refugees in Africa*.)

Our main pedagogical objective must be to bring the stark facts of the refugee phenomenon as rehearsed above into significant relationship with the pupils' own capacities for empathy and sympathy with this dire human plight. An appeal to collective and personal memories can be most promising. First, it is simple to point out that all refugees suffer the fate of being cut off from their origins, both in the sense of being uprooted from a familiar environment and also not infrequently of being parted from parents and grandparents—a twofold deprivation of nourishment essential to healthy growth—a traumatic experience with quite incalculable consequences for the behaviour patterns of the succeeding generation as it strives to come to terms with transit camp and host community. Such experiences only too readily become the sources of rancour and resentment towards all parent-authority figures. This can then be exploited by those in any society bent on recruiting personnel for the creation of social upheaval. By means of a well-known psychological mechanism, children are destined to live out for better or worse the unlived-out parts of their parents' lives. The frustrated and persecuted refugee parent tends to produce the aggressive and neurotic refugee child. Skilfully treated in the classroom, this aspect of the refugee phenomenon can help pupils to understand by means of reference to their own homes and parental relationships the importance of such deprivation of "reassuring liaison" with their past for refugees and the need to provide them with opportunities for striking new roots.

Coming next to the second of our archetypes, the shadow cast by and/or falling on that which is considered evil, primitive, the inferior function, it soon becomes clear that by definition the refugee must himself cast a very long shadow indeed and himself provide a fitting object on which the shadows of others can rest. As a man or woman who has been rejected, expelled and forced to flee by those of his own homeland, however hard he or she may consciously strive to accept their lot, a dark and bitter hatred must be given off from them on to their oppressors, and, if these are no longer within their reach, on some other persons available to play the role of scapegoat. Similarly the refugees themselves must constitute the object of the host country's or the transit camp commanders' anger or annoyance at being forced to deal with these strangers in their midst—these outsiders, many of whom neither wish to be assimilated into new surroundings and some of whom may be unacceptable in them. Conversely, just as in psychological parlance the "shadow" if properly understood and treated can act as a gold-mine, so the refugee, if thoroughly understood and appropriately treated, can bring rich benefits to his new country of adoption. Huguenots and Jews spring instantly to mind as examples.

What of the heroic image in connection with refugees? Often a refugee is one who has made heroic sacrifices for his beliefs on grounds of conscience, has acted as leader and comforter of his people on their way through concentration camps into exile, has become a distinguished ornament of the society which has adopted him. The problem itself has created its own heroes, a Nansen, Count Bernadotte or Sadruddin Aga Khan or the hundreds of obscure relief workers, who have laboured on their behalf in the field and in offices. For the pupils to be helped to recognise this type of heroism as evidenced in the work of governments and voluntary organisations is to contribute to the building up of a relevant image of the contemporary hero—he, who as refugee triumphs in adversity, he who out of his greater resources of power brings succour to the refugee in his calamity. The refugee's journey both resembles and differs from the traditional journey of the

THE PROMISE OF COLLECTIVE MEMORIES

hero: he is separated from his origins, but for a long time is not initiated into any new society and may indeed never return to his actual previous home or vicariously find himself once again at home elsewhere.

Because of the close proximity in which many refugees are huddled together for long periods of time, in conditions wholly different from those to which they are accustomed, personal relations take on an unusual intensity. The images of man and woman are vividly constellated: demands made by him of her that she should be his healing mother, beautiful princess, perfect mistress, and by her of him that he shall be the wise father with all the solutions, the gallant prince, the romantic squire-fantasies as contrasted with fact—these are more liable to be indulged in indiscriminately by refugees divorced from their norms of sexual behaviour. How vital to understand that where all has failed, political loyalty, religious conviction, economic self-sufficiency, the refugee tries to escape from futility into the at any rate interim fulfilment of love-relationships. These themselves, because they are often only escape-mechanisms or because they are nipped in the bud by separation due to a striking of the camp or a sudden chance of emigration to the other side of the world, fail to provide lasting satisfactions to those involved in them. Then again there may be marriages or liaisons between the refugee and a partner who belongs to the host country—a situation also fraught with difficulty because of the jealousy it can arouse in many different quarters.

For adolescents in school it may well be that by means of this particular double image of the male and female principle, they can gain the greatest insight into the intimate hopes and fears of the refugees. For they will be experiencing "falling in love" and can ponder that ineffable state as it takes place inside a refugee community.

It is when we come to consider the last of our archetypes, the Self or the primordial image of wholeness, that the very essence of the refugee's predicament is reached. Its nature is such as to precipitate that ultimate human crisis where bodily and mental needs have been in considerable measure met, but when the refugee begins to question the worthwhileness of his rescue. Has he been through so much, endured such an anguish of suffering, felt so agonisingly the pain of man's inhumanity to man that the very thing which constitutes his humanity has been crushed out of him? Here it is that the tale must be told of those thousands of gallant refugees who have not only endured material deprivation and intellectual stagnation and triumped over them both, but who in so doing have achieved an integration of their personalities, so that they have emerged from their ordeal more whole or holy than before. To commune with such a man or woman, to encounter the richness of his humour and compassion in the face of all his fellows' follies, can be a decisively educative experience for a boy or girl growing up in the world today. Such a refugee is not only the symptom of a disease but the witness to a promise of its care.

By this kind of study in depth of the refugee phenomenon pupils of varying ages and aptitudes can be related intellectually and emotionally to a problem of world order. They could be asked to conclude their study by examining the following text and then, from the generalisation it offers, discover specific case histories from the refugee situation in different parts of the world and report on them to their peers and to the teacher. Although this passage obviously refers to an early phase of the post-1945 period of the refugee problem its validity is not out of date.

The Man from the Hut

The huts stand, on the edge of a small village, built first for German soldiers, then used by Poles, they now accommodate refugees from East Germany. They hold five times as many people as the village itself. From one of them a man emerges. Forty-five years old, with grey hair, he has a look on his face which at first gives the impression of ironic laughter. But as though frozen stiff, his face never varies. The man once had a wife, two children, and numerous relatives. He possessed a home, owning a well-stocked farm. He possesses now—that is to say, he possessed three years ago for he used to be a soldier—nothing but what he is carrying on him. No more and no less. He has a wire contraption with a palliasse and a military locker which he shares with two other men. Five men are living in his room in the hut.

The man has a roof over his head, a bed and a third of a locker. He has work. He works eight hours a day building roads at 78 pfennigs an hour. He earns 34 marks 32 pfennigs a week. He has food. Occasionally he gets hold of a bit of old clothing, or some home-grown tobacco. One cannot say that society's provision for him has failed, and the man himself does not complain. Indeed, he speaks only occasionally, recalling his house, farm and stock, his parents, wife and two children. In so doing, he blooms like a flower and grows livelier. From being a "has-been" he becomes a person again. He comes to life only in a dead world, for it is a world that exists now only in his memory. He does not speak for long, however, but slides back into his silence always ending with the same question:

"Well, tell me, who am I then, and what am I living for, and what is the sense of it all?"

He expects no answer. The question hangs about him frozenly as the look on his face.

The state cannot answer it, for the state knows only such concepts as Levelling of Burdens, the Creation of Work, Land Reforms, and Small Settlements. But none of this is what the man means.

Society cannot answer it. Society has knowledge only of things like Care Committees, Goods Collections, Refugee Aid and Emerging Equalization. But none of that is what the man means. In the state's world and the world of Society the man is a registered number in an enormous card-index. Yet he is a living entity and an individual human being putting a quite concrete question: Who am I, for what purpose am I living and what is the sense of my existence?

The four other men living in the same room with him put the same question. It hangs like a cloud over the whole camp, over the whole country, over the whole continent really without expectation of an answer, yet there is a trace of expectancy in it, a suspended 'perhaps' which some day might receive an answer. (Hans Zehrer, *Man in this World*, Hodder & Stoughton, 1952.)

Education for world understanding can help to provide the answer to that perhaps.

2. THE MALAISE OF VIETNAM

The malaise of Vietnam is caused by over twenty years of warfare within her borders. This has been due to internal strife and intervention from outside. Before attempting a pedagogical interpretation in depth of that pitiable history, we need to recall its salient features. These are that the people of Vietnam have an ancient culture and system of government of their own and that from 1860 they came under French colonialist rule, against which during the 1920's and 1930's there were sporadic, nationalist outbreaks. The spearhead of these was the Vietnamese Communist Party under Ho Chi Minh, paralleled by the less militant Vietnamese Nationalist Party after 1927. In 1940 the Vichy regime in France collaborated with the Japanese, whereby the latter took over the country in the former's name, then turned against and overthrew the French in March 1945, but were eventually themselves overthrown at the end of the Second World War hostilities. The Emperor, Bao Dai, who had then succeeded to power, subsequently resigned in favour of Ho Chi Minh in August 1945. On 2 September 1945 he issued a Declaration of Independence, but by March 1946 the French had reasserted their claims, and their nominee, Ngo Dinh Diem, became theoretically ruler of the whole of Vietnam. However, war against his regime did in fact continue right on from 1946 to 1954 under the anti-French and ideologically aligned resistance leadership of Ho Chi Minh in the North.

In 1954 by the Treaty of Geneva a compromise was arrived at with the division of the country into South and North Vietnam. For two reasons this could not and did not last: one was an internal one, namely the mounting dissatisfaction with the ruling elements in South Vietnam, which resulted in the formation there in 1960 of a National Liberation Front and also the continuing subversive pressures on the situation from North Vietnam: the other was an external one, namely United States economic, diplomatic and finally military support for the South Vietnam government against what was proclaimed to be a take-over bid by Ho Chi Minh with the Communist Great Powers, U.S.S.R. and China, behind and supporting him. Hostilities grew larger and fiercer with the organisation inside South Vietnam itself of a resistance movement, the Vietcong, supported since 1964 by the North Vietnamese—the Viet Minh. By 1966–7 a full-scale war was being waged, a countryside ravaged, and the two cities of Hanoi in the North and Saigon in the South became the symbols of a vast, world-scale ideological encounter. This is staged in a tiny Asiatic area, the inhabitants of which, mostly poor and ignorant peasants, continue to suffer the appalling afflictions of an apparently endless war. In the words of a letter to *The Times* of 1 June 1967 there is a globally mounting "sense of outrage at a war in which such increasingly hideous means are being used to effect so very ill-defined and questionable an end".

Our interpretation must deal with the nature of that end: is it the national liberation of the Vietnamese? If so, from whom? Is it the defence of Asia and the "free" world against a Communist totalitarian menace? Is it, by any chance, the improvement in welfare of the population of Vietnam, North and South, as a whole? How far do the means employed by both sides to the conflict aid or impede the attainment of all or any of these ends? These questions are a measure of the sense of involvement in Vietnam felt by thousands, who themselves are far removed from the field of battle: they indicate that the Vietnam issue is a kind of tragic epitome of present human folly. This was conveyed in the Royal Shakespeare Company's production in London of "US"— a teasing play on the words, America and ourselves.

In presenting the malaise of Vietnam to his pupils the terrestrial teacher will establish its main factual features in some such style as above and point out that there are here involved legacies of an ancient civilisation, the imperialism of a European power and, most recently, the clash of ideological giants. Penetrating more deeply he can seek to show the ways in which men's primordial images of their origins, environment and ultimate destiny can be detected beneath the particular Vietnamese versions of them. For instance, it can be pointed out how for the majority of the native inhabitants their view of and hold on reality are still dominated by the images they form of the sources of their nourishment, the crops which feed them and the agencies, whether human or divine, that seem to determine their yields. The authority-figures of old-style mandarin, new-style commissar, the juxtaposition of barbaric violence and polite recreation as evidenced by a tennis tournament conducted within a stone's throw of terrorism at Hue—these alone can be taken as examples of the archetypal patterns of parent, lawgiver and lover. However, it is when the religious and ideological factors come up for treatment that the archetypes of "shadow" and "Self" are most clearly constellated.

Obvious adversaries abound here—North and South Vietnam as each other's shadows, the "Reds" as the shadows of the Americans, the "Yanks" as the shadows of the Communists, the Roman Catholics as the shadows of the Buddhists and vice versa. Here too are the integration motifs: the self-realisation of the National Liberation fighter, the crusader making the ultimate sacrifice of his very life for the cause of Communism or anti-Communism, the man or woman of goodwill seeking after honourable compromise in a transcendence of the conflict and often only suffering crucifixion in its pursuit.

It is surely not without significance that the clearest lead into a reverent understanding of the Vietnamese disease, itself a symptom of global malady, has been given by a Buddhist. (See *Vietnam: Lotus in a Sea of Fire. The Buddhist Story*, by Thich Nhat-Hanh, S.C.M. Press, 1967.) For it is by means of a rediscovery of the validity of the immanent experience of ultimate reality via the fusion of traditional Eastern wisdom and Western depth psychology that the strength can be regained which man requires if he is to transcend the otherwise irreconcilable opposites.

Let us briefly consider a few points taken from that book, all of which could be worked up into suitable lesson-material for the pupils, who are anxious truly to understand and therefore not to disagree with but to suffer with the people of Vietnam. The author begins by telling "how the Venerable Thich Quang-Duc burned himself in Saigon on 11 June 1963 to call the attention of the world public to the sufferings of the Vietnamese people under Ngo-Dinh-Diem's oppressive regime". He points out that this self-immolation had "a far greater emotional impact on the West than on the East because of the great difference in religious and cultural backgrounds". This act could only have been performed by either a madman (and all the evidence suggests that Thich Quang-Duc was kind, lucid and sane) or by a person so utterly convinced of the indestructibility of spirit as to be able to lay down his life unconditionally as a witness to what man is really for and a protest against what he can be made to do against his fellows. To what kind of value, the pupils might be asked, was he testifying? Then the class might be issued with copies of the following passage taken from a footnote in Thich Nhat-Hanh's book (pp. 66–7):

> Communism has a basis of social and personal idealism, and recruits thousands of men and women passionately concerned to eliminate the exploitation and inequality that have characterised much Western society, and to create a form of social organisation whose slogan will be "from each according to his ability, to each according to his need". This is an objective consistent with the best in most of the world's great religions, and with which religious men can have no quarrel. Moreover, the economic organisation of society in socialist terms, meaning one in which the means of production are operated for the good of the people generally rather than for the profit of a minority is consistent with the needs of a country like Vietnam. Few Vietnamese Buddhists or nationalist leaders could believe that their country could afford a Western-type capitalism even if they thought it was a moral form of social organisation. Vietnamese anti-Communism stems from the methods that organised Communism uses to attain its ends. . . . For many of us, however, for whom the stated objectives of Communism are largely acceptable, the opposition we feel grows from our conviction that when such methods are used to attain these "good" ends, the ends themselves become unattainable because the methods used corrupt the whole struggle. If humanistic religion has any meaning at all, it is that humanistic ends cannot be achieved by inhuman and depersonalising means.

The pedagogical exercise would then be to get the pupils to list the humanistic ends for which both sides claim to be striving, to compare and contrast them, and to inquire how far they are being contradicted by the inhuman and depersonalising means employed whether by Vietcong or G.I. Conclusions drawn from such a study will be a necessary first step to the preparation of constructive alternative policies.

More useful teaching material with regard to the actual plight of the Vietnamese peasant could be taken from pages 76 and 77:

> Whom would you follow: the Government of South Vietnam or the National Liberation Front? They replied: "We do not follow either. We follow the one who can end the war and guarantee that we can live." The peasants are not concerned about ideology, no one can frighten them with stories of the evils of Communism. With their property already destroyed, they do not fear that the Communists will take their property. And if one speaks to them of freedom and democracy, they say, "Of what use is freedom and democracy if one is not alive to enjoy them?" So it is clear

> that the first problem of the Vietnamese peasant is a problem of life itself: how to survive in the midst of all the forces that threaten them; how to cling to life itself.

Finally on page 88 the author writes:

> In such circumstances priests and nuns cannot go on preaching morality: the war has destroyed not only human lives but all human values as well. It undermines all government structures and systems of society, destroys the very foundations of democracy, freedom and all human systems of values. Its shame is not just the shame of the Vietnamese but of the whole world. The whole family of mankind will share the guilt if they do not help to stop this war.

To feel that shame is another step in the process of education for world understanding: it can be aroused by considering such problems and by perceiving from a specific instance what needs to be done within the general framework of analysis and prescription outlined in the Introduction to this book. Practically this means the reconvening of the Geneva Conference on the basis of the acceptance of a North–South partition of Vietnam, the re-establishment in Saigon of a Popular Front government, internationally promoted and guaranteed, and eventually the establishment of a Federation of New Indo-China, i.e. including Laos and Cambodia. Vietnam contains a rich promise of the collective memories of mankind concerning food needed, loyalties stretched and animosities transcended. The malaise of Vietnam is a symptom of globally sick mankind's attempt at cure—the cure being its recognition at a conscious level of the constants it previously held in common unconsciously, and its triumph over the no longer legitimate variables as illustrated by the agony of the Vietnamese.

3. THE PREDICAMENT OF UNO

It is entirely fitting that this book should conclude by asking and trying to answer the question so insistently posed whenever the world scene is discussed—why does not UNO or something like it work, when it's so clearly needed? Dag Hammarskjöld stated the reason incontrovertibly in an article in the *United Nations Review*, Vol. IV, No. II (May 1958):

We should recognise the United Nations for what it is—an admittedly imperfect but indispensable instrument of nations in working for a peaceful evolution towards a more just and secure world order. At this stage of human history, world organisation has become necessary. The forces at work have also set the limits within which the power of world organisation can develop at each step and beyond which progress, when the balance of forces so permits, will be possible only by processes of organic growth in the system of custom and law prevailing in the society of nations.

The key phrase in this passage is "The forces at work have also set the limits within which the power of world organisation can develop at each stage". It is precisely the task of education for world understanding to study these forces, not only at the political and economic levels, as has been attempted in previous chapters, but also at a deep psychological level, where the promise of human collective memories of co-operation may be redeemed. Philip Seed provides us with a valuable clue in his thoughtful study *The Psychological Problem of Disarmament* (Housmans, 1966). Pondering the problem of why it is that men and nations have so far failed to do what their own best self-interests demand, he diagnoses it as being due to psychological dissociation. He points out (pp. 44–5) how the incompatibility of the hope of international peace or friendship

"with the widespread use of nuclear weapons can lead to a problem of guilt which is resolved partly by a process of dissociation. In reality, the individual can claim legitimately that he is not personally associated with the weapons his State possesses. The hope of peace and the expectation of toughness which prevents a realisation of this hope, co-exist, side by side, dissociated. . . . Weapon systems are planned which will come into operation seven or ten years hence, while negotiations are conducted about a comprehensive disarmament treaty. . . .

There is always a danger that the twin ideas of disarmament and re-armament, peace and toughness, will feed into one another so that the hope of disarmament can actually help to promote the arms race. Governments meet the pressure of peace hopes by taking part in disarmament negotiations and by belonging to the United Nations, and then, when peace hopes fail, when negotiations break down or the U.N. fails to settle a dispute peacefully, a fresh impetus is provided for the pressure embodying the expectation of toughness. A renewed justification is found for re-arming, the paranoic fear is confirmed and the need for toughness vindicated.

In a later passage, which echoes Hammarskjöld's diagnosis, Mr. Seed writes:

> Although a feeling of world community is growing, it has not reached a point when the world is a community in which a supra-national system of law and government can operate. A distinction must be made between the inter-dependence of states, economically and politically, and a community. A community is partly sustained by political institutions, but institutions cannot be stabilised in the first place without a large amount measure of community whose people "have learnt to communicate with each other and to understand each other" (Karl Deutsch, *Nationalist and Social Communication*, p. 65, 1953). There is a fundamental difference between a community in the positive sense, and a common interest. A common interest does not by itself prevent the occurrence of wars.

It could be said that education for world understanding consists id transmuting common interest into community, a task which involves the clarification and purification of underlying and often, until revealed, unconscious motivation. Such a process can never come about unless public opinion becomes sufficiently aware of its own motives by understanding how it is being got at to resist the kind of infection contained in the following episode.

This extract from the *Sun* newspaper of 29 March 1967 is a particularly blatant and absurd illustration of the way in which the popular press can indulge its public's taste for mock heroics, scapegoatism and the projection of its often deep-seated self-hatreds. It is only necessary to substitute for the oil-tanker, *Torrey Canyon*, any one of the fashionable national or ideological bogies to perceive how the mechanism works: "In the end the *Torrey Canyon* met the classic fate of an enemy of Britain: she was put to death. The killing was watched by about 2000 people at Land's End, 16 miles away." Here there is a positively animistic attribution of diabolic powers to the empty wreck of a ship leaking oil into the ocean—an occurrence which, however regrettable and unpleasant, bears absolutely no relation to the villainous foreign power which is conjured up as the perpetual menace to Britain's virgin shores.

The latest example of UNO's predicament in the Arab–Israeli war in the Middle East reveals quite crudely the reasons for her impotence. They are that unless the Great Powers share an interest and a desire to enable UNO to function as a police-force, it cannot so function, but also that at any rate in the first place they do share an interest and desire to the extent of refusing themselves to become involved in a direct confrontation which could escalate into global war. Our educational message is surely this, that prudence and calculation may suffice to keep national chauvinism and economic rivalry in check for a time, but that these alone will not serve to transmute common interest into community and that without community a peace maintained by UNO cannot come about. The essential factor that needs to be added is the healing of that psychological dissociation, which we have seen to be the cause of mankind's inability as yet to inform UNO with an appropriate amount of collective psychological integration.

In terms of the psychological premises adopted in this chapter this means educating a sufficient number of men and women, the future international civil servants and keepers of the peace, to recognise in themselves and in others the archetypal constants and their periodical variables in the transaction of world affairs and then to be able to stand for the versions of those variables, which are legitimate in ensuring the evolution of world order. These are an authority rooted in an institution of supra-national government, which has achieved a balance between the positive and negative emotional tones of the archetypal parent figures: a heroic image compounded of the attributes of men and women dedicated to the solving of the world's food and population problems: a treatment of men's inferior functions, their shadows, not by projecting them but by accepting them in themselves: a love morality based on the sanctity of the "I–Thou" relationship, and finally shared values derived from a common recognition of that which constitutes the core of being a man or woman.

The nature of UNO's predicament, which we have been trying to probe, is well expressed in the following description of the role of the Secretary-General as summed up by Herbert Nicholas in *Encounter*, 10 February 1962: "He has become a politician without ceasing to be a civil servant, he is a Pope without a church, a conscience expected to establish justice but only on the explicit understanding that the heavens are not made to fall in the process."

Education for world understanding consists in building a church in which men of all faiths can worship and in nourishing a conscience recognisable as being that of the human race.

APPENDIX

A PEDAGOGICAL EXERCISE IN THE PRESENTATION OF AN HISTORICAL CONFLICT SITUATION

St. Thomas More and Thomas Cromwell

ENGLISH society at the beginning of the sixteenth century, expressing its dynamic through the organs of certain powerful groups and individuals, was becoming aware of itself as a national unit, was experiencing a change-over of its economic centre from baronial to merchant class and religiously was claiming more and more for the right of individual conscience—a claim which became associated with independence of Papal control and an embryonic secularism, which was, however, for many years yet to take the form of authoritarian Protestantism. It was the case that this complex received a personal focus in the character of King Henry VIII, to whom both of his victims stood in warring relationships.

More and Cromwell were both men very much of their period, but they came into conflict partly because of almost irreconcilable differences in personality-type, but even more because the former tried to embrace the future without becoming alienated from the past, while the latter assaulted the future without respecting the past. Both paid with their lives for the cause they championed: both were right and both were wrong: neither had more than fleeting glimpses of the underlying nature of their conflict.

By comprehending something of the tragic quality of the encounter between the two men, students of it can increase their own understanding of the structure of human personality. Particularly is this the case if Cromwell is presented—at least in part—as the

"Shadow", "the blind spot", "the inferior function" of More, projected on the stage of Tudor politics. History and personality are thus used pedagogically to illuminate and reinforce one another.

Having assimilated his facts and clarified his viewpoint—a process that must inevitably involve him in measuring the psychological types of More and Cromwell as against his own and his pupils with the aid of analytical psychology—the teacher will be ready to plan a time-table and select material for the manifest content of the various groups of children with whom he will be concerned.

Three types of pupils will now be considered:

A. Pupils of less than average ability—ages 14–15.
B. ,, ,, more ,, ,, ,, ages 13–14.
C. ,, ,, ,, ,, ,, ,, ages 16–18 (not History specialists).

Instead of postulating arbitrarily so many hours of curriculum space available for this study during one school term, the assumption will be made that an average of three hours a week is the time given, not counting such free-time activity as may be devoted to acting, modelling and painting.

Manifest Content and Latent Significance

A

I. *Manifest Content*

1. A simple account in story form of the struggle between two men, Thomas More and Thomas Cromwell (written especially for this purpose by the teacher, duplicated and distributed to each child), e.g.

"Four hundred years ago, when King Henry VIII was on the throne of England, there lived and died two remarkable men, called Thomas More and Thomas Cromwell. The story of the struggle between them is exciting, because it is about a problem with which we are all of us concerned every day of our lives, namely how do we decide between what is right and what is wrong, and how, having decided, do we carry out our decision?

"More and Cromwell were high-up officials and advisers of King Henry VIII, who, you will remember, wished to get rid of his first wife, Catherine of Aragon, in order to marry a girl called Anne Boleyn. Some of his reasons for wishing to do this were good, more were bad, and he quarrelled with the Pope about it so much that after a while he claimed that he, Henry, was head of the Church in England and not the Pope. This meant that he could decide for himself that it was all right to divorce Catherine and marry Anne, which he proceeded to do.

"Then he announced that everyone must agree with this and was backed up in his demand by Cromwell. More, however, refused to take the oath of agreement, because he thought Henry had done wrong: he was arrested, lodged in the Tower of London, tried for treason and finally beheaded by the King's orders.

"Being a great, wise and good man, but also a very human one, he had to overcome two faults in himself before he could face the ordeal honestly. One was pride, and the other was fear: both were rubbed into him by his enemy, Cromwell, who tried to shake his resolution by playing on these two weaknesses. But the very way in which he behaved helped More to recognise and repair these faults by humble submission to the God whose law he acknowledged as just—a divine law, which he declared in one of his finest remarks just before his execution: 'The King's loyal servant, but God's servant first.' One of the things More's life-story does is to make us ask the question: how in fact do we know when we are right?"

2. A reproduction of Holbein's *Portrait of More*. A reproduction of the Bodleian Library picture of Cromwell.
3. R. J. Unstead, *Great Tudors and Stuarts* (People in History, Vol, 3, Black, 1956), pp. 5–13 and 126.
4. Model of Tower of London (Traitor's Gate) with background of Tudor London constructed by the class.

II. *Latent Significance*

What is being asked of this group of children is to focus their attention, which will not be intellectual for the most part, on a certain episode in the past of their people. That episode contains one or two perennial problems of human motivation, illustrated by a particular and highly dramatic instance. The teacher may decide that these children cannot be expected to learn in such a way as to retain as part of their mental storehouse more than three facts:

1. A long-ago royalty and his ministers had a serious quarrel in London. (Names: Henry VIII, More, Cromwell.)
2. London looked very different then from nowadays, but the Tower stood and stands.
3. People quarrelled about some things that were the same then and now (women) and some things that were different (religion), but then as now there is the same problem of conscience.

In working with the class to an elucidation of these three matters, the student-teacher should be trained to use the theme of Cromwell as More's enemy, so handling it that while never making overt references to the mechanism of the "Shadow", some intimation is conveyed to the children of the nature of opposites by means of which they can begin to learn how to bear the enemy that is always within and without themselves.

B

I. *Manifest Content*

1. Mary R. Price and C. E. L. Mather, *A Portrait of Britain under Tudors and Stuarts (1485–1688)*, illustrated by R. S. Sherrifs (Clarendon Press, Oxford 1954).
2. A. Manning, *The Household of St. Thomas More* (Everyman, 1906), Extracts.
3. Morna Stuart, *Traitor's Gate*. An historical play in three acts (Collins, 1939), Extracts.

As well as more formal work a class debate with the motion:

"That in the opinion of this house Cromwell rather than More was the best representative of England's interests in the year 1534–5."

II. *Latent Significance*

In addition to the greater quantity of factual knowledge and understanding of issues, which might legitimately be expected of this group of children, the occasion should provide opportunity for the teacher to initiate them quite specifically into the tragedy of human conflict. This could hardly be better accomplished than through the medium of the play *Traitor's Gate* by Morna Stuart, use being made of extracts from Act III, scene 2, pp. 107 to 114, and Act III, scene 3 in its entirety.

Such extracts will, of course, have been led up to by ensuring that the class has obtained a clear, though necessarily simplified, impression of
- (a) the background of Tudor England;
- (b) the nature of the struggle, political, economic and spiritual, in which the main actors in the drama were involved;
- (c) the life stories of More and Cromwell down to 1534;
- (d) the significance of "the King's Matter" and the royal, perhaps national, need for assent to the Oath acknowledging Henry's supremacy over Church as well as State;
- (e) the unsavoury role of Solicitor-General Rich in particular.

"For the last time, will you sign?" says Cromwell to More in Miss Stuart's play (p. 107), and this leads on to the dramatic dialogue between the couple, in which the dramatist with great skill shows up the two chinks in More's armour—his vanity and his cowardice, both of these, of course, below the level of his consciousness until forced into his awareness by his "Shadow"—his enemy, Cromwell.

> "*Cromwell*: I do not like men of the world, who are saints, nor believe in them. I will confess to a certain human pleasure in exposing a self-lover in Thomas More of Chelsea." (pp. 109–10.)

A few lines later More remarks to Cromwell:

> "Only you have known where the tragedy of this play has lain, and from the bottom of my heart I thank you. . . . You are the only man whom I have never take in. I should prefer your admiration to any in the world." (p. 111.)

Nevertheless, as it is made quite clear, this does not mean that More is to give way, to surrender his position, but merely that he is now free to anticipate courageously a resolution of the conflict at another higher level.

> "*More*: I cannot live where the law of God is gone (i.e. an England when away from Rome)—I go to the absolute, the only heaven." (p. 117.)

The dependence of the one personality on the other is finely depicted in the lines:

> "*More*: Will you pray for me?
> "*Cromwell*: I never pray.
> "*More*: Then I must pray for you." (p. 114.)

A further extract presents More, in fear of death, visited again by Cromwell in the Bell Tower, who brings him his sentence of death but not, as More had been dreading, by drawing and quartering but by the more merciful axe.

> "*Cromwell*: The King will not shame you nor try you beyond your strength.
> "*More*: No. The King will not shame me, nor try me beyond my strength—so He lets me stand in my place below His monk and His priest." (p. 122.)

Again the dramatist exposes movingly the way in which More has learnt the truth about his own character, when he is made to say to Cromwell:

> "You shall be my living altar; and it is not unjust." (p. 123.)

The whole thrilling issue is nobly summed up in one final extract of dialogue:

> "*Cromwell*: The world shall not know that your mind was not at one with your conduct. How will you help them, if you confess it?
>
> "*More*: How shall it fail to help the world if they know that God chooses cowards also—and even cowards love Him better than themselves in the end?
>
> "*Cromwell*: Your time had not yet come. Often a man's call comes faintly at the first, like a false dawn and then dark—presently, from the east it comes at him again and it is day. If the struggle came late, it has ended—as it should. I have your forgiveness in the honour that I know when I am near you." (p. 127.)

As a result of their study of the manifest content of the history of More's and Cromwell's parts in the Reformation, illuminated by the light shed by the dramatic extracts which they have heard, as suggested by the few selections given here as examples, and sustained by the teacher's own inward participation in the spiritual struggle, the class will have learnt a truth about the nature of human existence in a dimension different from that of reason. This is a truth, which in later years must become explicit to them as they learn to come to terms with their own "inferior functions", the "shadow" side of their spirits' fleshy incarnation. Then the experience of having "done the Reformation" at school as outlined above must stand them in good stead, for they will be able to call on it, some more, some less consciously, for solace and inspiration.

C

I. *Manifest Content*
   1. *The Mirrour of Virtue in wordly Greatness or The Life of Sir Thomas More Knight by William Roper* (London, 1907 Edition).
   2. R. W. Chambers, *Thomas More* (London, 1945).

3. *More's Utopia*: edited by H. Osborne (London, 1936).
4. A. Cecil, *A Portrait of Thomas More: Scholar and Statesman* (London, 1937).
5. A reading and, if possible, production of the whole of *Traitor's Gate* by Morna Stuart.

A long essay to be written by each member of the class: "More was on the wrong side of History." Discuss this statement.

II. *Latent Significance*

All that need be said in connection with this group of considerably older and intelligent pupils is first that the onus of getting up the background reading must be placed squarely on them; secondly, that the teacher can devote himself to two matters, supervising the production of the whole play of *Traitor's Gate* and towards the end of the time available for the study expounding explicitly the psychological mechanism of the "Shadow", and the excellent example of it provided by the relationship between More and Cromwell.

SUGGESTIONS FOR FURTHER READING

BARRACLOUGH, *An Introduction to Contemporary History* (Watts).
BOLAM AND HENDERSON, *Art and Belief* (Hamish Hamilton).
BROWN, N., *Life against Death. The Psycho-analytical Meaning of History* (Routledge & Kegan Paul).
CAMPBELL, J., *The Masks of God* (Secker & Warburg).
CAMPBELL, J., *The Hero with a Thousand Faces* (Pantheon Books).
DUNN, TED, *A Search for Alternatives to War and Violence* (Clarke).
HAMMARSKJÖLD, DAG, *The Servant of Peace*. Hammarskjöld's speeches edited by Wilder Foote (Norstedt & Söners).
JUNG, C. G., *The Development of Personality* (Routledge & Kegan Paul).
SEGAL, *The Race War* (Cape).
STORR, A., *Human Aggression* (Penguin Press).
WATERLOW, C., *Tribe, State and Community* (Methuen).
Year Book of Education 1964: *Education and International Life* (Evans).

INDEX

Algeria 51–2
Amfortas, wound of 6
Apartheid, a teaching problem 95–8
Armaments 18–19
Art, its transcendent function 25

Belief, a teaching problem 37–40

Consciousness, evolution of 4–9
Cuba 102

East–West dilemma in teaching 101–5
European Common Market 20
European Community schools 90–2

Food supplies 3, 74

God, location of 43
Government, teaching about 32–4, 40–1

Language learning 29
Latin-American Free Trade Area 20

Malawi 48–9
Materialism 58
Mexico 49–50

Moscow classroom 96–100

Nationalism
  definition of 45
  European expansionist
    Britain 48–9
    France 51
    Spain 49
  ideological
    China 54
    U.S.A. 54
    U.S.S.R. 54
  pocket
    Cuba 55–6
    Eire 55–6
    Switzerland 55–6
  renovated
    Egypt 52
    India 53
    Israel 53
    Japan 53
Novels as teaching aids 77–83
  Camus' *The Fall* 81
  Forster's *A Passage to India* 81–3
  Mann's *Dr. Faustus* 78–80
  Musil's *The Man Without Qualities* 76–8
  Pasternak's *Dr. Zhivago* 80–1

Politics, their transcendent function 20–4
Primordial images
  of the hero 111–14
  of the lover 114–18
  of the parents 106–11

Primordial images—*cont.*
  of the shadow 118–23
  of the spirit 124–5

Race relations 21–2, 35
  in the Midlands of Britain 87–90
Refugees
  in Middle East camps 92–4
  as world phenomenon 126–39
Religion, its transcendent function
  26–7

Science
  its trancendent function 25–6
  teaching about it 34–7, 41
Spanish Civil War 23, 49
Sport, its transcendent function
  26, 72

Taboos 38
Teachers, their quality and status
  84–7

Trade, its transcendent function
  18–20

UNESCO 12, 85–6
United Nations Organisation 3, 16, 23
  its predicament 144–8
Universities
  diagnosis of 59–62
  function 62–3
  and world order 64–9

Values, shared 39–40
Vietnam, malaise of 139–44
Voluntary organisations 41

War, its transcendent function
  14–17
Workers, solidarity of 22–3
World Congress of Faiths 27
World Council of Churches 27
World Law Fund 67